Dealing with the
CUSTOMER
FROM HELL

A SURVIVAL GUIDE

SHAUN BELDING

Publisher's note

Every possible effort has been made to ensure that the information contained in this book is accurate at the time of going to press, and the publishers and authors cannot accept responsibility for any errors or omissions, however caused. No responsibility for loss or damage occasioned to any person acting, or refraining from action, as a result of the material in this publication can be accepted by the editor, the publisher or any of the authors.

Previously published in Canada in 2004 by ECW Press, 2120 Queen Street East, Suite 200, Toronto, Ontario, Canada M4E 1EZ entitled *Winning with the Customer from Hell*

First published in Great Britain in 2005 by Kogan Page Limited entitled *Dealing with the Customer from Hell*

Kogan Page Limited
120 Pentonville Road
London N1 9JN
United Kingdom
www.kogan-page.co.uk

British Library Cataloguing in Publication Data

A CIP record for this book is available from the British Library.

ISBN 0 7494 4451 7

Typeset by Saxon Graphics Ltd, Derby
Printed and bound in Great Britain by Creative Print and Design (Wales), Ebbw Vale

This book is dedicated to:

Don, for your wisdom;
Jack, for your vision;
Gene, David and Diane, for your support over the years
(maybe, if I sell enough of these things, I can finally pay you
back);
Gary, for your continued encouragement;
Yvette, for believing that the 'for better' part still may actually
come true;
and Dad, wherever you are, for teaching me that anything can
be a hammer.

Contents

Introduction: to hell and back again

What a lovely day. You know, if I do nothing else today, I think I'm going to make some poor sod's life miserable.

The Customer from Hell. The favourite topic of working people everywhere. Reports of this notorious monster can be heard daily in canteens, restaurants and offices across the country. The air is filled with outrageous, absurd and sometimes terrifying tales of a barely human, impossible person who preys indiscriminately on unsuspecting salespeople and customer service people. Like emotional vampires, these people drain us of all positive energy and replace it with feelings of frustration, anger and hurt.

You do know whom I mean, don't you? People who are waking up in the morning, stretching, looking out the window and saying to themselves, 'What a lovely day. You know, if I do nothing else today, I think I'm going to make some poor sod's life miserable.' Then they sit there and, over their breakfasts of cold gruel, carefully plan their strategies for systematically ruining your day.

But who are these people? What are they really thinking? Why do they do the things they do? Why do they seem to have such a profound impact on our lives? More importantly, what can we do about them?

I've had the great pleasure of meeting and working with many thousands of people in the past few years from virtually every walk of life. And, of the hundreds of seminars I've conducted, I don't think one has gone by without someone asking, 'How do you handle difficult customers?'

Not long ago, a young woman who worked as a part-time salesperson for a chain of stationery shops recounted to me in painful detail a truly horrendous customer-contact experience. A man had come up to her, incensed that the store didn't have adequate wheelchair access. He had cursed at her. He had shouted at the top of his lungs. Nothing she had said to the man seemed to help.

How vivid was her memory of this man? Well, she was able to describe to me exactly what he looked like. She remembered the clothes he was wearing. She remembered what his voice sounded like. She even remembered the scent of his cologne. She was able to reproduce their conversation word for word.

As she told me her story, her voice became increasingly strained, and her shoulders began to slump. I listened and watched with fascination as she relived the emotions of the moment. This customer had become real to her again, surfacing to spoil another day. She was visibly shaken.

What I found most disturbing was that the unpleasant scene she was recounting had happened more than six months earlier. How many thousands of customers had she seen in the meantime? How many thousands of positive customer experiences had she had over those six months? Yet this one awful experience had stuck with her like a wad of chewing gum to a shoe, affecting both her personal motivation and her day-to-day performance.

I suspect that anyone who has worked in sales or customer service for more than a month has had at least one of these encounters and has experienced the same kind of trauma. Some of the stories I've heard would curl the toes of the most grizzled veterans. To be honest, as much as I hate to admit it, there was a time when I made light of these kinds of stories and the impacts that Customers from Hell can have on our emotional well-being. 'These people represent probably less than one-tenth of

1 per cent of the people we deal with', I would think knowingly. 'Aren't we better off concentrating on the 99.9 per cent of our customers who are pleasant to deal with?'

I have since come to realize that, while it is true that Customers from Hell represent just a tiny fraction of the customers we deal with, it is equally true that this small group profoundly affects how we feel about ourselves and how we interact with our other customers.

Customers from Hell can be broken down into two basic categories: unsatisfied and unreasonable. An unsatisfied customer is one who has either positive expectations that are not met or negative expectations that are met. An unreasonable customer is one with unreasonable expectations of either you or what is acceptable in his or her own behaviour.

When these expectations are met – or not met, as the case may be – and conflict arises, unsatisfied and unreasonable customers can exhibit a wide range of behaviours that most of us find unsettling at best. These behaviours can include belligerence, swearing, lying, negotiation, verbal abuse, whining, impatience, shouting, demands on your time, condescension and other equally pleasant responses.

Most Customers from Hell appear, at first glance, to be acting unreasonably. What we will discover as we explore the actions of these customers, however, is that unreasonable and inappropriate behaviour does not necessarily mean unreasonable expectations or an unreasonable person. Most often what you, as the service provider, experience is an unsatisfied customer behaving in an inappropriate manner.

You see, most Customers from Hell are no different from you or me. They don't belong to some evil Customer from Hell cult, and they're not really going out of their way to get you. Basically, they're pretty decent people whom you've just been privileged to catch at their worst. Can you honestly say you've never said or done things you've regretted later? Who is the Customer from Hell? Look into the mirror the next time you're having a bad day. What are these customers really thinking? They probably think they are the victims, not you.

But why do Customers from Hell affect us so dramatically? Well, for starters, sales and customer service jobs are exceptionally stressful occupations. If you work full time in an average shop, for example, you're going to come face to face with some 20,000 to 50,000 customers every year. If you're the receptionist in an office, you might see and talk to over 100 people a day. A professional sales representative might be dealing with customers who are worth millions of pounds to the company. Those are big numbers, and it is an awful lot of humanity for anybody to have to cope with. It's not hard to understand how someone seemingly intent on adding unexpected stress to our lives might push some of us right over the edge.

Basic psychology also plays a large part. Our actions and emotional states are dictated largely by what we focus on. If we focus on the positive things in our lives, we tend to be happy. If we focus on the negative things, we tend to be unhappy. This is a simplification, of course, but a truism nonetheless. Unfortunately, given a choice between focusing on positive things and focusing on negative things, human beings have a strong tendency towards the latter. Our attention is typically drawn to the exceptions, not to the rules.

If you don't believe me, try this experiment just for fun. One evening ask a friend or spouse to list five things that went wrong that day. Five negative things. Five things that could have gone a little better. Within a minute or two, you will have your list, and it will likely not be restricted to just five items. Then ask the same person to list five things that went right that day. Five good, positive things that happened. Notice how much longer the second list takes to complete – if it gets completed at all.

The media have known about and exploited this quirk of human nature for years. Dozens of newspapers have attempted to develop a 'good news' format, only to have it quickly perish. Human nature. Think about it. It's no surprise, then, that personal traumas stick with us for a long time.

So, does this mean that people are just negative by nature? I don't really think so. It's just that negative events seem to be, for some reason, a lot more memorable to us. But why is that? Why are Customers from Hell so memorable? Why do we experience that gnawing, gut-chewing anxiety when we encounter them? Why are these situations so stressful?

The answer is experience or perhaps lack of experience. Most of us have never before had a real need, or an opportunity, to learn skills for coping positively with people who behave badly. Think about it for a moment. When you were growing up, didn't your parents spend most of their time teaching you concepts such as sharing, respect, love and caring, among others? In school, didn't your teachers work on concepts of teamwork and responsibility? At work, aren't you told to smile and sell? For the most part, we are taught how to interact positively.

We usually learn how to deal with conflict, however, by trial and error, and as a result our solutions are rarely productive. Some of us have learnt to strike back, to flee or to sulk. Some of us cope by crying, shouting or snapping back. The truth is that most of us have never learnt the skill of resolving conflict in a positive manner. In fact, most of us just don't experience conflict frequently enough to practise coping with it positively.

We're also not used to negotiating from the position of underdog – unless you happen to have been a playground bully's favourite target. Like bullies, Customers from Hell typically have an agenda that is different from our own. Their goal most often is to 'win' – either emotionally or substantively. Our goal is customer satisfaction, which can be a very tough pill to swallow when the 'satisfaction' sought by Customers from Hell appears outrageous and unreasonable.

You can't win against a Customer from Hell – it's not possible. Of course, you certainly don't want to lose either. Fortunately, it is possible, in most cases, to win with the Customer from Hell – to resolve a situation to everyone's satisfaction. The answer is much simpler than you may think. Not easy to execute, mind you, but the principles are simple. You really just need to fine-tune and focus your active listening skills and develop proactive, positive language skills.

In *Dealing with the Customer from Hell*, I will present some proven methods for managing difficult situations and customers. But before we get into the good stuff, perhaps I should clarify what this book is not. Unlike many other conflict resolution strategies that have been developed, this is not a simple personality-based approach. Many of the techniques presented in other books and programmes focus on various behaviours exhibited by the people whom you are in conflict with and offer methods for responding to each. People are categorized into personality types, and each type is given a name and a strategy.

There is no question but that personality plays a role in conflict. And, as a result, a fundamental understanding of people and their personalities is an important part of the equation. An understanding of personalities is particularly relevant with 'environmental' conflict (eg coping with a colleague). But I believe that in situational conflict, such as with customers, personality is only one of many elements of which we need to be aware. More important, I'm not convinced that, when conflict with a customer arises, any of us really has the ability, in the heat of 'battle', to analyse the other person's behaviour instantly and respond appropriately and constructively.

While the goal of this book is to help you to work better with difficult customers and situations, the principles, skills and tips outlined are not restricted to that use only. Although I focus on people in sales and other customer-contact jobs (all of whom I refer to as 'service people'), what I cover is powerful communication skills that have a wide range of applications beyond conflict management. This book concentrates on a universal six-step procedure that, when executed properly, will help you to resolve the vast majority of difficult situations in which you are likely to find yourself. Each step introduces skills that apply equally to family, friendship and business relationships.

The book also offers solutions for specific situations that cannot be resolved using the six-step process. But I think you will find that these situations and the customers they involve are, thankfully, few and far between.

Finally, remember that, to actually make it work, you will need to practise and rehearse the techniques actively and take a painfully honest look at any of your own idiosyncrasies that contribute to conflict. The principles in here work, I can promise you that. How well they work for you depends on the depth of your commitment to changing your approach to conflict.

1

Customers and their expectations

Some think you're an idiot; some think you're a hero.
Some expect the best; others expect the worst.

Have you ever noticed that Customers from Hell seem to appear out of nowhere? One minute you're merrily minding your own business, and the next you have some lunatic screaming in your face. Have you ever asked yourself 'What is her problem?' or 'What has got into him?' or 'Why does she act that way?' Of course you have.

Unfortunately, we tend to ask these questions after the customers have hung up or walked away. If we took the time to find the answers while the customers were still around, we would resolve many of these conflicts with a lot less headache. The answers to these questions tell us a lot about why our Customers from Hell behave the way they do – what they expect and what has created these expectations. And, as you'll discover, an understanding of expectations plays a huge role in how well we respond to these situations.

All customers you meet bring with them a set of expectations. These expectations are created by their needs, circumstances, past experiences, personalities and personal situations. Most have positive expectations, but some have negative and even unreasonable ones. With the majority of customers, these expectations do not create any particular challenges for us. Occasionally, however, they will have a significant effect on a customer's behaviour.

Let's take a look at some of the positive, negative and unreasonable expectations customers may have, starting with positive expectations:

- They believe you have what they need.
- They think you will be able to solve a problem.
- They believe you will care.
- They expect you to be professional.
- They believe your products or services will be reliable.
- They think you will be trustworthy.
- They believe their business is valuable to you.
- They expect you to be cheerful.
- They expect your prices to be fair.
- They believe you will stand behind your products or services.

Now let's look at some negative expectations:

- They believe you will be unskilled.
- They expect to get a hassle when they have a problem.
- They believe you do not care.
- They expect you not to have enough authority to handle a situation.
- They think you're going to try to take advantage of them.
- They believe your product is of poor quality.
- They think your product is overpriced.
- They believe you're interested only in a quick commission sale.
- They expect you to be grumpy.
- They think their business is not very important to you.

Finally, here are some unreasonable expectations:

- They believe you should accept sexual or racial harassment.
- They think you should accept unruly behaviour from them or their children.
- They expect you to deal with them under the table.
- They think you can spend a lot of unproductive time with them.
- They believe they are always right.
- They think you should accept physical threats or bullying.
- They think you have been trained to take advantage of them.
- They expect you to cater to their every whim.
- They think they are more important than all of your other customers.
- They believe you, personally, are responsible for all of their problems.

No two customers, it seems, have identical expectations of you or your business. Some customers like you immediately and become loyal, while others take an instant dislike to you and become cool and distant. Some think you're an idiot; some think you're a hero. Some expect the best; others expect the worst.

As I've suggested, many factors contribute to these expectations. They fall into five basic categories: needs, personal situations, circumstances, personalities and predispositions.

Customers' needs

Every customer you come into contact with has a need. For most, it is a positive need that ultimately leads to a purchase. Customers from Hell often have different needs, however. They need to return merchandise. They need to let you know that they may have paid too much for something. They need reassurance. They need to see a demonstration of something before they buy it. They need to make somebody else happy with their purchase. They need to purchase something that is out of stock. They need a bargain.

A 'negative need', such as having to return something or being in a hurry when there's a long queue, is an obvious breeding ground for conflict. But even a 'positive need', such as having to purchase a gift for a niece's wedding, can result in conflict if that need goes unfulfilled. These needs, both positive and negative, are established long before you come into contact with your customer. They are very real, are totally beyond your control and play a significant role in generating conflict.

You may not want to hear this, but a significant amount of our suffering with Customers from Hell is self-induced. Often we, not the customers, unwittingly plant the seeds of conflict. As I will discuss in greater detail later on, one of the common mistakes made by well-meaning salespeople is to misinterpret a customer's need, and this misinterpretation can create frustration and lead to conflict.

One spring, for example, I set out to purchase a new set of golf clubs. Now, I should point out that the only thing keeping me from a career as a professional golfer is that I'm useless at the game. I love it with a passion, but it has never loved me back. I thought, though, that maybe I could begin improving my game by improving the equipment I was using. Problem was I really had no idea how to select a set of clubs. I needed expert advice.

My first stop was a reputable golf shop that carried a large selection of clubs. I had no sooner entered the shop than a smiling young man approached me and offered to help. He led me through the aisles of bags, carts and other unidentifiable (to me) stuff, and then gestured to a wall displaying no fewer than 50 sets of clubs.

'Here they are', he announced proudly, and then stepped back to let me look around.

Overwhelmed, I confided to him that I really had no idea what I was looking for and would appreciate some suggestions.

'Of course', he said obligingly. 'Approximately how much did you want to spend?'

I explained to him that money wasn't really an issue but that I wanted a good set of clubs that would serve me well. This seemed to confuse him a little.

'Well, they're all good clubs', he said finally. 'Some of them are just engineered a little differently.'

That's a big help, I thought to myself; then aloud I asked, 'Well, what, for instance, is the difference between this set for £1,400 and that set for £250?'

'Oh, well, the £1,400 set is made out of different material and weighted a little differently, that's all', he replied without hesitation.

'Oh, OK', I said uncertainly. I migrated to the more expensive clubs, working on the assumption that they would be better quality.

I was handling a £1,100 set when the salesperson chirped, 'We do have a set on sale right now – regularly £450, now on for £350. It's a great bargain.'

'Really?' I said, without a lot of enthusiasm, and then followed him to the clubs. 'Are they as good as those £1,100 ones?' I walked back to the more expensive sets.

He ignored my question and instead told me of another set of clubs, also on sale for £350. Again I looked at them, and again I walked back to the other clubs. Twice more during our encounter he dragged me away from the more expensive sets to offer me the low-end products. I ended up walking out in quiet frustration.

The young salesperson lost a sale and completely frustrated me because he failed to listen to and acknowledge my needs. I wanted a good-quality set of clubs that suited my purposes; he wanted to sell me a cheap set. He assumed I was looking for a bargain. He assumed my needs were the same as his or perhaps the same as his previous customer's. That misinterpretation and my ensuing frustration could easily have led to a confrontation. Fortunately, because I'm just such an all-round wonderful person, all that happened was that he lost a sale.

Customers' personal situations

A former colleague of mine, whom I had worked with for several years, was once faced with a gut-wrenching conflict of loyalties. A disaster had occurred with a major project she was working on for one of our clients. To correct it, she and her entire group were going to have to work well into the night. To make matters worse, that evening she was supposed to embark on her long-delayed honeymoon. Her plane tickets were non-refundable, and even a reimbursement by the company could not remedy the fact that her husband would be unable to recover his holiday time.

While she was brooding on her predicament, she was approached by her CEO. He began to discuss minor corrections to some work she had done on an earlier project. She exploded and launched into a 20-minute tirade that was heard throughout the office. Until that time, I had never heard her raise her voice, lose her cool or say an unkind word to anyone. But we all have a threshold – even those of us who are wonderful.

One of the great truths of life is that at any given time we are all under some degree of stress. Sometimes that stress is positive and productive; other times it is negative and destructive. The nature and degree of this stress play large parts in our daily behaviour.

Fortunately, the personal situations of our customers don't often significantly affect our dealings with them. Someone may be a little grumpier or happier or quieter than normal, but it's usually not enough to distress us. When one of our customers is experiencing an extraordinarily negative situation, however, and enters our domain with the corresponding stress, it may not take much of anything to trigger erratic behaviour.

A negative situation can include personal trouble with a husband or wife, a divorce, the loss of somebody close, the loss of a job, the stress of a job and so on. Many of us have experienced financial stress: a bounced cheque, a rejected credit card, a broken-down car with no money to fix it. In fact, there are as many different kinds of stress producers as there are people. Some people can experience intense stress simply by discovering lint on their clothing. Others can go through disastrous situations seemingly unfazed.

It has been said that customers have become more demanding over the past few years, but I'm not sure that 'demanding' is the right word. Apprehensive maybe. Certainly more cautious. But why shouldn't they be? The world is becoming an increasingly stressful place in which to live, and that stress affects everything we do.

As salespeople and service providers, we have no control over our customers' personal situations. Nor do we, in any real sense, have any way of understanding their personal situations before we come into contact with them. We need to remember, though, that a customer's personal situation can, and often does, play a significant role in conflict. Even the most pleasant people, when caught in a desperate position, can react badly.

The circumstances

The very circumstances of your contact with a customer can be the cause of conflict. Perhaps a hurried customer is forced to wait in a long queue. Maybe a customer simply can't afford to purchase a desperately needed item. Maybe you need a manager's authorization to process a return, and the manager is at lunch. Maybe the customer's credit card is up to its maximum credit. Maybe the warranty a customer is calling to enquire about expired two weeks ago.

Sometimes the unpleasant circumstances we find ourselves in are caused by a customer service person (maybe even you) not having done his or her job properly in the first place. Sometimes the circumstances are a result of ill-conceived company planning and policies. No-return or exchange-only policies in shops, as I will discuss towards the end of the book, just beg for conflict. Hotel restaurants are notorious for being understaffed, resulting in excruciatingly slow service, which in turn results in conflict. Some jewellery shops make a practice of hiding price tags (to force customers to approach salespeople), which inevitably irritates people.

But even with the best of companies, awkward circumstances can arise: the computer system goes down; an unexpected throng of customers shows up when you're understaffed; a thousand calls come in when all the staff are on their lunch breaks. It seems to be a part of life. Whatever the cause of the circumstances, it's the person on the front line who is faced with the dissatisfied customer.

What makes these circumstances especially difficult is that they are typically stressful for both the service person and the customer. Sometimes the overwhelming temptation for you is to say to your customer, 'Look, this isn't easy for me either!' (not a recommended strategy). More often than not, the customer has a legitimate right to be dissatisfied. And while you very well may have a right to be dissatisfied too, you can't make that your customer's problem.

Whenever I hear salespeople insisting on 'standing up for their rights' when they are with a customer, I think of a wonderful old saying:

> Here lies the body of Johnny Grey,
> Who insisted on taking his right of way.
> He was right, dead right, as he sped along,
> But he was just as dead as if he were wrong.

Recognizing and defusing potentially negative circumstances

Some circumstances are natural breeding grounds for conflict. Sometimes the conflict is inevitable, but often we have the opportunity to minimize it with our very first words and actions. Here are some of the negative circumstances in which we commonly find ourselves, as well as some strategies for minimizing the conflict.

Declined credit card

You've rung up the purchase. The customer is standing in front of you, and there are two people behind waiting in the queue. You swipe the credit card through the machine, and the card is declined. What do you do?

If you are like most people, you say one of the following.

▦ 'I'm sorry, but your credit card has been declined.'
▦ 'Ummm, there appears to be a problem with your credit card.'
▦ 'I'm sorry, but you are going to have to use a different method of payment.'
▦ 'There seems to be some sort of problem... Let me just try it again.'

None of these strategies is as productive as it could be, and each has the effect of embarrassing your customer. These strategies make difficult circumstances worse.

The customer may now feel compelled to explain what's happened or, equally likely, will express outrage that the card was declined. The customer might direct his or her emotion at you. Even though the customer might have been expecting the card to be turned down, he or she will try to minimize the embarrassment by attempting to convince you (and the other customers around you) that there has been a Terrible Mistake. Truth be told, most of us have a pretty good idea when our credit cards are getting close to the edge. And, though your customer may be embarrassed by its being declined, chances are he or she is not going to be all that surprised.

You will never be able to eliminate your customer's embarrassment completely, but you can minimize it, and any ensuing conflict, by trying one of the following approaches instead:

▦ Hand the card back and say quietly 'Do you have another card you would prefer to use?'

- Hand the card back and say quietly 'We've been having a little trouble with our machine lately. Do you have another card you would prefer to use?'
- Hand the card back and say quietly 'Oh, these stupid machines! Do you have another card you would prefer to use?'

In each of these examples, the salesperson maintains control by asking a question of the customer. Specifically, the question is designed to direct the customer to a positive action. The second and third examples are intended to provide an 'out' to help the customer preserve his or her dignity. Any one of these approaches will help to minimize a stressful situation.

No-refund policy

A shop has a no-refund policy, but a customer is returning a product and wants a refund. The typical salesperson's responses are the following:

- 'I'm sorry, exchange or credit note only.'
- 'We don't give refunds. You will have to exchange it.'
- 'I'm sorry, but it says right on your receipt that there are no refunds.'
- 'I'm afraid we have a bit of a problem – we have a no-refund policy.'

These are classic examples of negative language. You're always better off trying to present things with a positive spin:

- 'Our shop has a terrific exchange policy. What have you seen that has caught your eye?'
- 'Unfortunately, the shop doesn't give cash refunds – but we do have a great exchange or credit-note policy. What have you seen that has caught your eye?'
- 'I'd love to refund this, but this shop has a great exchange or credit-note policy instead. What have you seen that has caught your eye?'

As with the example of the declined credit card, I'm recommending that the salesperson gently outline the situation and then take control by asking a question of the customer. Doing so helps to direct the customer to make a proactive decision.

When you fail to take control – when you say something such as 'I'm sorry, exchange or credit note only' without following it with a question – the unintended implication is 'So what are you going to do about it?' This is at best an unproductive response and at worst a confrontational one.

Unusual delays or long queues

Your customer is in a hurry and has had to wait in the queue for 10 minutes before being served. You're a waitress in a busy restaurant, the kitchen is running a little slow and people are starting to get a bit irritated. You've been in a meeting and just discovered an urgent phone message from a client that was left three hours ago.

Typically, when faced with these situations, service people focus on increasing speed and efficiency. The sales assistant puts her head down and concentrates on the cash register in the hope that the customers will realize she is, in fact, working as fast as she can. The waiter rushes the order to the table when it's finally ready and slings the plates into position. The law clerk begins to talk at a faster rate and higher pitch to communicate that she's been busy. Faces screw up and harden; voices become clipped and mechanical; body language screams out 'I'm working as fast as I can, but don't you dare mess with me. I could just lose it!'

This may sound a little odd, but one of the great secrets of customer service is that, when people are in a hurry, the last thing you should worry about is how fast you are going. I learnt this lesson from Elaine, a friend and former employee in one of my toy shops. Elaine is, without question, one of the most highly skilled 'people persons' I have ever had the pleasure of meeting. She is a tremendous salesperson and was an invaluable asset to my company. Her only 'weakness', so far as I could see, was that she had very little patience for things even remotely mechanical. Pocket calculators were a minor challenge; the phone system was a constant source of stress for her; and she almost quit when I brought in a computerized cash register system.

Elaine was working alone in the shop one late November day. Two other employees were having lunch, and I had disappeared to meet a supplier in a restaurant. Shortly after I arrived at the restaurant, the manager came over and told me that I was needed at the shop. 'Apparently, the cash register isn't working', he said.

As I quickly walked back to the shop, I envisioned a frantic Elaine facing down a Christmas rush of impatient and unpleasant customers. When I added to that the stress of a misbehaving computerized cash register, I fully expected to find her curled up in a foetal position in the middle of the shop.

As I got closer, I could see through the entrance more than a dozen customers queuing at the cash register. I had a vivid image of what Elaine's letter of resignation was going to look like. But to my great surprise (and delight), I saw as I entered the shop that the customers were anything but grumpy. Quite the opposite, in fact. I felt as though I had walked into a party.

Elaine, instead of trying to hide from the problem, had decided to manage it by entertaining the customers. She had them joking with each other and laughing out loud. By the time I arrived, she was in the process of walking up and down the queue soliciting suggestions on words to describe the computer. Everyone was having a great time.

When Elaine spotted me marching towards her, she announced, in a voice loud enough for everyone to hear, 'Shaun, we have decided that the following best describes your stupid computer: it is unreliable, ignorant, rude, offensive, rubbish… and stupid!' While everyone was laughing, Elaine turned to me and said under her breath, with deadly seriousness, 'Fix the damn thing!' She then turned back to the troops and continued her entertaining while I got the computer up and running again.

(It turned out she had simply forgotten to hit the Enter key, but I never had the heart to tell her!)

Elaine made the best of a bad situation. So much so, in fact, that customers were still joking about it years later.

What would most of us have done? We would have just stood there, apologizing to the customers, letting the stress build up. We'd have panicked. Some of us would have got angry. The lesson I learnt that day is that customers are far more interested in how well they are treated than in how quickly they are processed.

You don't have an advertised item in stock

The featured item in your company's sales brochure didn't show up on time. The supplier didn't send the full shipment. The manager didn't order enough. Whatever the case, you now have a steady stream of unhappy customers demanding to know how your company has the audacity not to have the advertised product in stock.

Here are some of the things I've heard from the mouths of service people:

- 'I just work here.'
- 'I don't know when they'll be showing up. You'll have to keep checking.'
- 'Sorry.' *(Shrugs.)*

Each of these responses suggests to the customer that it's the customer's problem, not yours, and each focuses on the negative aspects of the situation.

If you find yourself in this situation, try a proactive response such as 'I wish I could tell you I had one for you, but unfortunately the item hasn't shown up yet. Would you like to drop by tomorrow to see if it has shown up, or would you like me to give you a call when it comes in?' By asking such questions, you have re-established control, changing the customer's focus from the problem to a proactive decision.

Customers' personalities

Every interaction with a customer involves dealing with that customer's unique personality (not to mention yours). As discussed, this is often the focus of conflict management techniques. And it is, in truth, a significant factor in generating and resolving conflict.

Analysing an individual's behaviour is really the closest we can come to understanding his or her personality. As I've pointed out, however, an individual's behaviour during a conflict is not necessarily an accurate measure of his or her personality. Anyone can, at one time or another, exhibit unpleasant behaviour. In a three- or four-minute conflict situation, we might assess someone as a hostile-aggressive personality, when the person is actually a typically passive person in desperate need.

There are unquestionably highly effective and proven techniques for dealing with specific personality types. These techniques are appropriate for resolving ongoing conflict in the workplace, where you have the opportunity over time to gain a better understanding of a person. However, in a conflict situation with a customer, somebody with whom you may have had little or no previous contact, you do not have the time or enough information to make a judgement about that individual's personality. Even if you do have the skill and intuition to pinpoint someone's personality type accurately in two or three minutes, that's only part of the battle. You still have to develop a workable strategy for dealing with that personality type and plan the appropriate responses. This requires time that you simply don't have and planning that, in a stressful environment, is challenging indeed.

Perhaps the greatest mistake made in gauging the personalities of others is to assume that everyone else is, or should be, more or less like you. The last time I checked, there were several billion people on this planet, each with a unique personality. Your perception of someone's personality is not based on some objective, universal standard, because there isn't one. Your perceptions come directly from the viewpoint of your own personality. You may, for instance, perceive someone as over-sensitive, while that person may perceive you as insensitive. Who's right? Who's wrong? Neither of you.

Personality, nonetheless, is a significant factor in any conflict, so it is something that we, as service people, must be aware of. There will be times when, no matter what we do, a conflict we are handling keeps escalating. Personality is often the random element that can thwart your best efforts.

Customers' predispositions

The final piece of baggage customers carry with them is a set of predispositions or pre-existing beliefs. In other words, before customers have even spoken with you, they may have a set of ideas about either your business or you personally. Unfortunately, these ideas may not work in your favour. Customers may believe they're going to get a hassle, for example. They may believe someone who works in customer service will be too stupid to resolve a problem. They may think you are going to try to cheat them. They may believe you are not honest. They may believe you will agree with their selections only because you are paid to do so.

Have you ever anticipated having a problem with someone and pre-planned what you were going to say – your 'script' – before you met him or her? Of course you have. That's a result of predisposition. Predispositions can be caused by many different things, and like it or not we all have them. The most common types of predisposition are those we've developed through experiences. We draw conclusions from our personal experiences and then project those conclusions on to future events.

Let's say, for instance, that you're in a shopping centre and you enter three shoe shops in succession. In the first two shops, salespeople 'pounce' on you (or so you perceive), badgering you, leaving you with the sensation of what we call pressure. As you prepare to enter the third shop, how are you likely to be feeling? You may never have been in that shop before, perhaps you haven't even heard of it, but what is your emotional state as you cross the threshold? Apprehensive? A little fearful? What are you expecting from that salesperson walking towards you? Is it any wonder that customers will occasionally blurt out a frantic 'I'm just looking!' before the salesperson even says hello?

It doesn't have to take three or four repeated experiences for someone to develop a predisposition. Ever heard the phrase 'First impressions are lasting impressions'? We begin to establish an understanding of people, places and things the first time we see them. For some people, a single experience is all it takes to form a virtually unshakeable opinion.

We all have predispositions. Some are created by prior experiences. Others have been taught by teachers and parents. The extreme of predisposition is, of course, prejudice. Racism, sexism and ageism all affect our relationships with our customers. Think of the people around you – your friends, your family. What are their predispositions? Some people, for example, are predisposed to believe that a woman working in a high-tech environment will not have as much knowledge or expertise as a man working in the same field. Some women buying a new car are predisposed to believe that a male salesperson will not take them seriously or will treat them as if they are stupid. Some people are predisposed to believe that young people don't make good managers; some believe that older people don't make good managers.

Perhaps your customer has had an unpleasant experience with your company before or knows somebody who has. Maybe he or she has a distrust of men or women in your occupation. Perhaps he believes that all salespeople care about is making a quick deal. Whatever predispositions your customers have, they are real and can have a real impact on the way they behave.

When you think about it, what I've painted here is a bleak,

distressing picture. We haven't even met the customer yet, and here he or she is with a set of expectations that we don't understand and can't influence – is it any wonder that we find conflict so difficult and so stressful? Needs, a situation, the specific circumstance, a personality and a predisposition – these five elements determine whether the customer comes to you with a set of expectations that is positive or negative. These expectations, when combined with your response, determine whether there will be conflict and whether that conflict will become a confrontation.

The essence of resolving conflict is first to separate the expectations that lead to the conflict from the behaviour that fuels it and then to work to understand those expectations. Our natural tendency is to react to the customer's behaviour, which simply doesn't work. Conflict resolution means taking positive action, not waiting for the customer to leave before you ask 'What's that person's problem?'

The vast majority of the customers we see and talk to every day, the satisfied customers, generally have a positive set of expectations. They expect certain things of us and our companies, and we live up to those expectations. But even when your customer has positive expectations, conflict can arise if those expectations are not met. Here's the formula in a nutshell:

A negative set of needs, situation, circumstance, personality or predisposition creates a negative expectation.

A negative expectation, when combined with a negative response on your part, will create conflict.

A negative set of expectations with a positive response could have either a positive or a negative outcome, depending on the strength of your response. The same holds true for a positive set of expectations and a negative response.

Conflict begins with expectations. Your response determines whether the seeds of conflict take root, and the quality of your response depends entirely on your ability to understand those expectations.

2

A little introspection: preventative medicine

Before we start pointing our fingers at our customers, we want to make sure that the fingers shouldn't be pointed at us.

One of the recurring themes of this book is that many of the difficult situations we encounter need never happen. Most difficult situations are born of customers who are frustrated by unfulfilled expectations caused by misguided company policies, a shortage of skill or motivation on the part of service people, or simply a lack of customer focus in the company. It only makes sense that trying to avoid self-inflicted wounds should be your first goal. But before concerning yourself with how to handle Customers from Hell, let's make sure you're not creating them.

Many things within the control of managers and employees can ensure greater customer satisfaction and help to reduce conflict. Some are subtle, small suggestions, and some are large, sweeping policy issues. The more of these you can deal with up front, the fewer challenges you will have to deal with in the long run. To give you an idea of what I mean, I have outlined 18 things you and your company can do to maximize customer satisfaction. Work on the ones you can control, and encourage other people to work on the ones over which you have no control.

1. Become a better service person

Read Chapter 3, 'A salesperson's mission', a couple of times and encourage your fellow employees to do the same. If you are an employer, bring in a strong customer service/sales trainer or training programme. Make sure it is one that will have a measurable effect on performance. Try to avoid CDs, video-tapes, posters on the wall, buttons and fancy slogans. Bring in a programme that increases people's skills. The pleasant side-effect of training, of course, is that it can significantly increase your sales.

2. Have a hassle-free, money-back return policy

A good friend of mine has an immensely successful shop that does in excess of a million pounds in sales every year. He credits a good portion of that success to having changed from a 30-day exchange or credit policy to a completely hassle-free, money-back policy. An awful lot of unpleasant customer encounters are created by restrictive return policies.

Yes, I understand the rationale behind these restrictive return policies, but for the most part that rationale represents acute short-term thinking. An average customer uses a shop eight times a year and remains within a shop's target market for 10 years. That's 80 purchases. If each purchase averages £50, a shop will make £4,000 in sales from that one customer. To me, it doesn't make sense to risk losing £4,000 of business for a £50 item, not to mention the severe repercussions when upset customers express their discontent to their circles of friends. If you are in the business of selling things, your success will increase if you are also in the business of taking those things back.

3. Lose the negative signage

I remember pulling into a roadside restaurant after a long drive. As I pulled in, I noticed a big sign in the car park that said 'No Dogs'. Another sign 10 feet away warned 'Trespassers Will Be Prosecuted'. Ten feet from that was a sign that said 'No Buses'.

As I got to the front door, I noticed three more signs. One said 'No Shirt, No Shoes, No Service', another one said 'Toilets for Restaurant Patrons Only' and the last one said 'No Take-away During Busy Times'. Inside, at the cash register, another sign said 'No Personal Cheques'. Several months later, when I passed by again, there was a new sign at the front. It read 'Out of Business'.

A national park I was visiting one day had a spectacular mountain path with some of the most breathtaking scenery I have ever witnessed. What really took my breath away, though, was the experience of walking around a bend to find myself facing a 6-foot-high white sign with huge fire-engine-red hand lettering that read 'Don't Litter!' So much for 'getting away from it all'!

Sometimes we get frustrated that our customers aren't reading our 'rules', so we make our signs bigger and blunter, underline the noes and make bold our key points. The few customers who do read the signs will find them angrily written and highly offensive.

The truth is, most customers don't bother reading – they're busy looking at your stock, or your view, or you. If you think you must have certain signs, look carefully at the way they are worded. For example, a sign that says 'No Refunds, Exchange Only, Receipt Required' would be far better if worded something like this: 'We want our customers to be happy. If you have any problems whatsoever, bring in your product and your receipt, and we will be delighted to exchange it.'

Remember: negative signage creates a negative atmosphere, and a negative atmosphere nurtures conflict.

4. Remove 'You're going to have to' from your vocabulary

Be conscious of the way you say things to people. Customers don't have to do anything. There is always a better way to say things. (I will discuss this in more detail in Chapter 3.)

5. Don't start to close up shop early

Walk through a shopping centre 15 minutes before closing and see how many retailers have their doors half-closed. The signal to customers is clear: go away; you are a nuisance; we don't care. For the customer who is desperate to make a last-minute purchase in your shop, the 'you're not wanted' message might be the last straw.

6. Don't advertise things you don't have

Many companies believe that price is the biggest issue for today's consumers. That is not the case. A national survey conducted in 1995 ranked price third among customer concerns. In first place was poor customer service, and spot two went to a company not having what it advertised in a sales brochure. Be forewarned: customers expect to get what is advertised, and 'just in time' inventory systems are worthwhile only when they are, in fact, in time.

7. Never, ever promise something you can't deliver

Never let a customer have higher expectations for your product than the product can actually deliver. It's great to make a sale but terrible to lose a customer.

A bank branch once had the wonderful idea of having all of its employees wear badges that said 'Am I Smiling?' The thought behind it, of course, was to reinforce the concept of smiling to the employees. Unfortunately, as more and more customers encountered stern, surly-looking employees with an 'Am I Smiling?' badge, the end result was that the branch only became a great source of amusement and conversation.

8. Make sure your prices are clear

Many businesses, such as consulting companies and law firms, quote a flat rate 'plus expenses', with the expenses being an annoying tally of every photocopy and paper clip the company used on a customer's behalf. It is a recipe for frustration.

Retailers are continually using convoluted and confusing pricing games – such as Buy Two and Get the Third One for Half Price! – that only irritate customers when they end up not getting the kind of discount they were expecting. Some shops intentionally leave prices off their merchandise, in the belief that doing so will force customers to talk to a salesperson. This tactic is just as likely to frustrate them, causing them to walk out the door.

Set your price; make it clear; make it consistent.

9. Don't let the large print giveth and the small print taketh away

Avoid cutesy advertising and promotion at all times.

For a long time, personal computer manufacturers and retailers were advertising incredibly low prices for their computer systems. The small print, as you may recall, was 'Monitor not included'.

Advertising like this may sound very clever to you, but your customers will find it very deceptive – and rightly so. No one likes to feel as if he or she has been tricked. It may bring you business in the short term, but when you lose a customer's trust and respect you lose business in the long term.

10. Empower your employees

Give your employees the authority to make decisions on the spot. No customer enjoys being told 'You'll have to talk to my manager.' If you are entrusting an employee with the success of your business, whether that employee is full time or part time, why in heaven's name would you not give him or her the tools to do the best job possible? If you don't believe that your employees have the capacity to make good decisions, then you've hired poorly.

Yes, even your best employees will make mistakes when you empower them. And some of those mistakes will cost you money in the short term. In the long term, though, your customers, your employees and you will all be happier. Nothing is more productive than a strong, trusting work environment.

11. Don't let customers feel ignored

Probably all of us have heard at some point 'Please hold, your call is important to us... Please hold, your call is important to us… Please hold…' I think the reason that airline executives always seem so baffled as to why so many of their customers have a grumpy edge to them is because they don't have to buy their tickets the same way as the rest of us do. Twenty minutes or more of waiting in a telephone queue to book a flight might give them a whole new perspective on the seeds of air rage.

I remember once calling the help desk for some computer software I was using. I was on hold for 40 minutes, and then the line suddenly went dead. When I called back, I got the message that the offices were now closed and to call back the next morning. The time was 5.01.

I will never understand why companies have 'customer service departments' structured in such a manner that they can't adequately service their customers. If you want repeat business, don't let your customers feel ignored.

12. Don't create voicemail hell

I used to be dreadful at returning calls. That is, until one day the advertising agency I was working for almost lost a large client because of it. That was back in a time, if you can imagine it, before voicemail. Far too many people now use voicemail as a call-screening device, to the ongoing frustration of callers. There is no better way to start off on the right foot than actually to answer your phone.

13. Don't be the e-mail to nowhere

There is a company that produces website development software. Instead of having a freephone number, its technical support system is e-mail based. You send the tech support people an e-mail outlining the problem, and they, in theory, e-mail you back with the solution. I have sent off four e-mails in the past three years, and I'm still waiting for the replies.

Some people are simply dreadful at returning e-mail messages, causing no end of aggravation to their customers. But even those of us who are generally pretty good still slip up. Sometimes we get an e-mail from a customer, and we are so focused on dealing with the issue raised that we forget to respond to the customer. The customer, assuming that we have forgotten, gets upset.

As a general rule, when you get an e-mail from someone, respond to it instantly – if for no other reason than to let him or her know that you are doing something. Your customers will be much happier and much more patient.

14. Make appointments

Some salespeople like just to drop in on customers and prospective customers. 'The customer's not returning my calls,' they think, 'so I'll just drop in.' Sometimes the strategy works. Often, though, it results in customers never returning the sales-people's phone calls again.

A big part of customer service has to do with respect. Respect for customers' needs, respect for their time, respect for their space. When you want to see someone, make an appointment. It is far more respectful, and these days anything less is not acceptable. It may be a slightly longer process, as you navigate through voice-mail hells and e-mails to nowhere, but you are far less likely to get grumpy customers.

15. Keep appointments

When I was younger, I was chronically late. Not for business appointments or golf games, of course; but when it came to anything else – social events, meeting my wife, meeting my family and so on – I was always the one straggling in 15 minutes after everyone else.

It took my mother-in-law about 30 seconds and 10 words to teach me the lesson that decades of nagging couldn't. The family was gathered for a wonderful celebration dinner, and I, true to form, strolled in five minutes late. My excuse, as always, was airtight, but it didn't stop my wife from remarking on my chronic tardiness. I came back with my usual 'I'm not that bad. Besides, I'm always on time for the important things.'

'Well,' my mother-in-law said with a smile, 'I suppose that means we're not very important, are we?'

There I stood, facing the most important people in the world to me, and absorbed the words. I suddenly realized the message I had been sending to all of the people who had had to wait for me over the years. That moment ranks as one of the most poignant, and most embarrassing, of my life.

I'm not late very often any more, but in those rare times that I catch myself running late the words of my mother-in-law resound loudly in my head. There is no faster way to send the message 'You're not very important' than by being late for an appointment.

16. Dress for success

Unless you work in a call centre, in a very dark bar or deep in a mine somewhere, the way you dress is critical. I remember a service engineer coming into our house once to fix our phone lines. He had wrinkled trousers and a stained shirt that was coming untucked at the front. My instinctive reaction was 'You just don't care, do you?' Not a great message for a customer to receive at the very beginning.

17. Don't talk business at a funeral

Timing is everything. At the reception following a friend's wedding a few years ago, we found ourselves sitting at a table with Rick, the CEO of a large company, and his wife, Janina.

Drinks were flowing, people were dancing and everyone was having a great time. Rick and Janina had just returned from the dance floor when a man appeared at the table and sat down beside Rick. He handed Rick his business card and proceeded to begin pitching a new product to him. Rick turned to look at me, then at Janina and then back at the intruder. He pulled a business card out of his wallet, handed it to the man and said 'This is my number. Don't ever call it.'

There is a time for everything. Funerals, weddings (some people say they're the same thing), bar mitzvahs, birthdays and so on are not the time for business. Whenever possible, plan your interactions with customers. There is a time to talk business and a time just to build relationships. Bad timing can lead to angry customers.

18. Plan for success: 'If you're the waiter, how come we're doing all the waiting?'

Some restaurants never seem to have enough staff. Hotel restaurants are notorious for being understaffed both in the kitchen and in the restaurant itself. This always astounds me because they, more than other restaurants, should be able to predict how busy they will be from day to day. They have, after all, a captive audience and should know how busy the hotel will be at any given time. Even the best waiters and waitresses get angry customers when the customers have had to wait a long time for service.

I have watched large groups of customers just get up and leave when they feel they've been ignored for too long. When that happens, I always wonder if the owner or manager sits down to calculate exactly how much money has been lost for the sake of one minimum-wage employee.

To summarize, here are the 18 things you and your company can do to maximize customer satisfaction:

1. Become a better service person.
2. Have a hassle-free, money-back return policy.
3. Lose the negative signage.
4. Remove 'You're going to have to' from your vocabulary.
5. Don't start to close up shop early.
6. Don't advertise things you don't have.
7. Never, ever promise something you can't deliver.
8. Make sure your prices are clear.
9. Don't let the large print giveth and the small print taketh away.
10. Empower your employees.
11. Don't let customers feel ignored.
12. Don't create voicemail hell.
13. Don't be the e-mail to nowhere.
14. Make appointments.
15. Keep appointments.
16. Dress for success.
17. Don't talk business at a funeral.
18. Plan for success.

3

A salesperson's mission

The better the job we do as sales- and service people, the fewer challenges we have with customers.

OK, OK, I know – I'm supposed to be talking about Customers from Hell here, not sales- and service people. But I think it's important that we agree on what customers should be able to expect of us. A lot of the conflict encountered with customers would simply never happen if we just lived up to their expectations. Although this book is about managing difficult customers, I think we all know that conflict rarely has only one side to it.

So how can you be sure that it's not you who are causing the problems? How can you keep from unwittingly becoming the Service Person from Hell? What can you use as a benchmark to evaluate your performance in terms of your relationships with your customers? The term I have chosen to use, 'service person', covers a lot of ground. I define it as anyone who has contact with customers. A service person could be anyone from a lawyer, to a part-time shopworker, to a butcher, to a nuclear reactor salesperson. Is it really possible to establish universal benchmarks? I think that the answer, for the most part, is yes.

I believe that the job of a service person can be broken down into six different elements, six things that make the difference between really good service people and the plain, average service people we encounter every day. These elements contribute to what I think should be the mission of every service person: to provide the most positive experience possible to every customer with whom he or she comes into contact.

I have encountered many fine service people over the years, and if there is one thing common to all of them it is this sense of mission. It is the customer-oriented attitude. They never forget that the ultimate goal is always customer satisfaction.

All too often we find ourselves getting caught up in the mundane support tasks of restocking shelves, updating prospect lists, tidying, filing, doing inventory control, among a myriad of other things. We bring our personal problems to work. We begin to lose focus. We begin to take our customers for granted – or, worse, we begin to think of them as nuisances.

When I used to own a small chain of toy shops, I had a plaque hanging on the wall of each:

> This country has no resource greater than its children.
> No one has greater wealth than one who has a child.
> And there is no greater tragedy than a child who has been denied his or her future.
> If we can help just one child grow to be a better person,
> Then we have achieved our objective.
> If we can make just one unhappy child happy,
> Then we have made a profit.

I believed this adage when I wrote it, and I believe it now. Throughout all the challenges and stresses we face each day, we must never lose sight of our commitment to our customers. So what are the six key functions of a really good service person?

1. A service person sells.
2. A service person makes customers comfortable.
3. A service person is an ambassador for the company.
4. A service person is always positive.

5. A service person is always honest.
6. A service person cares.

Let's take a closer look at these key functions one at a time.

Function 1: A service person sells

Not all people in a service occupation are in sales, but, if you are, your first function is to sell.

Is this profound or what? In other words, we are not being paid just to stand behind a counter and wait for people to make their selections and hand over their money. We can't just wait for the phone to ring. We can't just wait for our customers to come to us. In today's highly competitive business environment, this is unacceptable, not just to our bosses, but to our customers as well.

You may consider selling to be a rather obvious part of a salesperson's job, but to many people – believe it or not – 'selling' is somehow considered inappropriate behaviour. Frightening but true. To be fair, the people who tend to feel negatively about selling really don't have a good handle on what selling is all about. They think of selling as something, well, unwholesome. They think of it as someone 'doing something' to someone else.

In retail, the role as salespeople who actually sell reflects a change from the way things used to be. In the past, we've used terms such as 'assistant', 'customer service representative' and 'consultant', and some companies even had the audacity to call their salespeople 'assistant buyers' (because the salespeople, of course, assisted customers in making good purchases). When I began conducting retail programmes many years ago, only about half of the employees who attended considered themselves salespeople. Fortunately, the attitude is now changing.

In commercial sales, there is a similar positive trend. Being a salesperson is becoming an honourable profession once again. It wasn't that long ago, however, that salespeople were operating under titles such as 'account executive', 'marketing specialist' and 'consultant'.

As a salesperson, you should assume that everyone who walks into your shop or agrees to see you needs or wants something. Everyone – even people who are 'just browsing' or 'just information gathering' – has a need or want. It may not be a specific need – it may not even be a current need – but something motivated them to get out of bed that morning and see you. They chose to turn to your company because they believe it has, or may have, the answer to that need or want.

In retail, one of the more common questions we are asked is 'What about when customers are just browsing?' It's a fair question. Think for a moment about your own routine. You've finished your shopping and have some time to kill. You begin wandering around the shopping centre, peering at the window displays. Some shops you don't enter, others you do. Since you don't have anything specific in mind, what was it that motivated you to turn into these particular shops? If you had friends with you, chances are they would not have been drawn to the same shops as you. What was motivating them?

We browse only in shops that attract us. And they attract us primarily because of the stock they carry – stock that we either typically purchase or aspire to purchase. We may not have an immediate need, or a clearly defined need, but it is there nevertheless, and salespeople should never lose sight of it. The same is true when prospective customers agree to see a company's sales rep. They may not have a current use for the rep's products, but they are seeing the rep because they think there may be a future opportunity.

One of the great limiting factors in sales today is that many salespeople work on the basis of assumptions that are neither proactive nor productive. For example, some salespeople believe that customers prefer to be left to their own devices, without a salesperson's 'interference'. Others assume that customers have absolutely no intention of buying. I'll never forget one two-hour coaching session I had with four middle-aged salespeople in a department store, trying to persuade them to say hello to their customers. They were adamant that their customers would find this a distasteful intrusion into their shopping experiences. Needless to say, this store – in fact the whole chain – has struggled.

What is selling?

We talk about 'selling', but what is it really? What, exactly, differentiates a salesperson who sells from one who does not? Selling can be broken down into four basic activities: creating a first impression, probing/discovering the customer's needs, presenting the perfect product and closing the sale. Different training programmes, of course, use different terminology, and some programmes include many more steps, but these four are the basics. The basics are what contribute the most to positive sales growth and positive customer experiences. And it is over the basics that salespeople are most likely to trip.

Creating first impressions

The first sales step, and therefore the first responsibility of a salesperson, is to create a positive first impression. In a retail environment, this means greeting customers – every customer who comes into the shop. They need to feel appreciated, and a simple hello from you can make all the difference in the world.

The concept of greeting a customer is obvious. It's almost so logical and self-evident that it doesn't warrant discussion. But as obvious as it may seem to you, I challenge you to walk through a shopping centre without passing dozens and dozens of salespeople who are task oriented – putting products on shelves, pricing items, walking around with clipboards – and thus totally ignoring the customers who pass them by.

All it takes to greet a customer is 'Hello', 'Good morning', 'Good afternoon' or 'Good evening'. But this has to be initiated by the salesperson, not the customer. It's not hard to do – there's no magic involved. Greeting customers is perhaps the simplest activity salespeople perform, yet research indicates that fewer than 30 per cent of employees in shops greet their customers well. Scary, isn't it?

In a commercial sales environment, creating a first impression involves careful attention to body language and dress. It also requires confident eye contact and a firm, warm handshake.

I'm not sure that there is any single social interaction that sends a faster and more powerful message about a person than the way in which he or she shakes hands. Some people do the 'limp fish'; others do the 'big crunch'. Both send the horribly unproductive message 'This may not be someone I want to get to know better.'

A good handshake is firm and constant, with the webs between the thumbs and forefingers meeting. While shaking hands, you focus behind the other person's eyes and give a warm, genuine smile. It is the best way in the world to make a good first impression.

Probing/discovering customers' needs

After greeting a customer, a salesperson learns as much as possible about that customer – to discover what the customer needs, why the customer called, why the customer is in the shop or why the customer agreed to see him or her. Through skilful questioning and attentive listening, the salesperson must determine not only the customer's intellectual needs, but his or her emotional needs as well.

Although this discovery process is one of the cornerstones of being a good salesperson, it is not as widely practised as it should be. The vast majority of salespeople are content to let their customers browse or, conversely, follow them around. Those who aren't ignoring their customers spend their time answering questions or spouting off reams of information instead of taking control (as the experts they are) and asking the questions that will determine their customers' needs.

Does the discovery process really make a difference? It certainly does. Take a look at how a typical sales interview might go without the salesperson probing to determine a customer's needs:

> *Customer: Do you sell flip charts?*
> Salesperson: No, I'm afraid we're right out.
>
> *Customer: Oh... Any idea where I might get one?*
> Salesperson: Well, you can try Paula's Presentation Palace. I know they usually carry them.
>
> *Customer: They're all the way across town!*
> Salesperson: Yes, I know. There may be somewhere closer, but I'm not sure where.
>
> *Customer: OK. Well, thanks anyway...*

Sound familiar? This is typical of many sales situations. The customer asks questions, and the salesperson does his or her best to answer them, but neither the customer nor the salesperson ends up with his or her needs satisfied.

Here's the same interview, this time with the salesperson discovering a little about the customer by asking a few probing questions:

> *Customer: Do you sell flip charts?*
> Salesperson: [Probing.] No, I'm afraid we're all out. What did you need it for?
>
> *Customer: Well, I'm doing a seminar today, and I realized that I've got nothing to write on.*
> Salesperson: [Probing.] Oh, you are in a spot. And the nearest place I know of to get a flip chart is right across town. Let's see... how do you typically use the flip chart?
>
> *Customer: I use it to write down the key points I make, so that those in the audience can then copy them down at their leisure. I just don't know what I'm going to do without one.*
> Salesperson: [Probing.] Does it have to be a flip chart?
>
> *Customer: What were you thinking?*
> Salesperson: Well, we don't have flip charts in stock, but we do have some whiteboard easels. You know, the ones that use the dry-erase markers? They're a little more expensive than a flip chart, but they'll do the same job.
>
> *Customer: That would be perfect. Can I take a look at them?*

The salesperson in the first example was polite, helpful and well meaning, but didn't take the time to understand the customer or that customer's needs. As a result, the salesperson lost a sale and forced the customer to drive across town for a solution available in the shop. The salesperson in the second example asked three simple questions, made a sale and saved the customer a lot of grief.

Customers usually have a pretty good idea of what their needs are when they come into your shop or give you a call – but they rarely have the wealth of product knowledge that you have. If you don't ask them appropriate questions – as a doctor does with a patient, for example – your customers can't benefit from your expertise.

A customer in one of my toy shops marched into my office three days after one Christmas and slammed a product down on my desk, furiously declaring it to be the absolute and totally wrong thing for her four-year-old child. She was livid, loud and very unpleasant. She had spent more than £100 on a product she had picked out herself, and her child's Christmas was, in her opinion, ruined. It was difficult to disagree. The toy was designed for a child 10 to 13 years old. By not adequately discovering the needs of this customer, the salespeople in the shop at the time she had selected the product had fallen down on the job – and the result was a spoilt Christmas for a little girl (and her mother). Did the customer have a right to be upset, even though she had picked out the product herself? Absolutely. Who was to blame? We were.

Presenting the perfect product

The third step of the sales process is for the salesperson to identify the perfect product based on what has been learnt of the customer and then to present that product to the customer. This requires a thorough knowledge of your products as well as their features and benefits. It is also the part of the process where the customer is depending on the salesperson to make a firm and appropriate recommendation.

Selling a customer the wrong product is a recipe for conflict. Nothing can dissolve a customer's trust in us faster than an exhibition of poor product knowledge or an inappropriate recommendation. I have suggested that perhaps the most common error salespeople make is to second-guess customers' needs. At the presentation stage of the sales process, we are in the most danger of paying the price of making inaccurate assumptions about people.

One of my company's clients was a national mobile phone service provider. I was coaching the salespeople in one of this client's shops when a man came in looking for a mobile phone. The customer was young, casually dressed in jeans and a T-shirt, and appeared to have little knowledge of the products. Even though the customer said that he required the phone for business and would probably be using it on a fairly frequent basis, the salesperson sold him a starter package that featured a low monthly base fee but had high airtime costs. The rationale for this, the salesperson explained to me, was that he didn't think the young customer would be able to support the higher monthly fee of some of the premium packages. When I pointed out that the premium packages offered substantially lower airtime rates, which would be more appropriate for someone who would be using the phone a lot, the salesperson responded, 'Yes, but he's young, and the young ones tend to use the phones more in the evening and at weekends, when the airtime is free.'

A couple of months later, I discovered that the customer had returned to the branch after receiving his first bill, extremely angry with the salesperson. His phone bill had been almost three times what it would have been had he received the right package in the first place. The salesperson had learnt the hard way a lesson about second-guessing his customers.

Closing the sale

The final step in the sales process, closing the sale, is unquestionably the least understood part. In the past, it was described as 'asking for the business' or 'getting the customer to sign'. It was viewed as the manipulative part of the sale, the point at which the salesperson 'got the customer to do something'. It's not surprising, then, that closing the sale has always been considered the hardest and least pleasant part of the sales process.

In truth, closing the sale is more about salespeople saying or doing whatever they can to determine whether the customer has made a purchase decision. It's not so much a matter of 'asking for the business' as it is of finding out if you're on the right track and bringing the sale to its logical conclusion.

Some of the best closing questions in the world are neither slick nor manipulative. Asking, for example, 'Is this pretty much the sort of thing you had in mind?' gives customers the opportunity to tell you how comfortable they are with your recommendation. More direct questions such as 'Which of these colours do you prefer?' help customers to focus on making a decision.

Unfortunately, few salespeople close sales well, if at all. Many don't recognize this as part of the sales function, don't realize how important it is or fear being perceived as 'pushy'. This fear is common, and there are a lot of aggressive sales-people out there. You will find when you look closely, though, that the uncomfortable, pushy part is due to the lack of questions asked to discover a customer's needs. Closing a sale, when done properly, rarely makes a customer uncomfortable. On the contrary, it is critical to creating a comfortable relationship with a customer.

I was on my way to a seminar with a business associate one snowy, blustery day in 1993. As we were walking from our hotel to the conference room, we passed a menswear shop. We had a little extra time, so we decided to go in and see what the shop had. It was an elegantly appointed, upmarket shop with beautiful merchandise. My friend headed straight to a wall of sweaters, while I was drawn to the selection of ties. On the rack was a tie that I had seen in Florida a couple of months earlier and had fallen in love with.

'Come here. Look at this', I called to my associate. 'This is the tie. This is the one I've been telling you about. This is the most beautiful tie I've ever seen. I want this tie.' Standing 4 feet away from me was the shop manager, listening to our conversation.

Trouble was I wasn't wearing the suit that the tie was to match. So I finally decided to forgo the tie for now and drop in later when I was wearing the appropriate suit. The manager just stood there and said nothing. I never got the opportunity to go back, of course, and to this day I have been kicking myself. The more I thought about it, the more I realized I would have bought the tie if the salesperson had closed the sale.

What were some of the (less than subtle) clues the manager got from me? 'This is the tie… This is the most beautiful tie I've ever seen. I want this tie.' Had the manager had the courage to simply say 'I agree. It's terrific. Would you like to look at some shirts to go with it?' I would be the proud owner of that tie. And after I expressed my concern that it might not match my suit, he could easily have outlined his return policy and offered to give me a refund if it turned out not to be a good match. As it was, I walked away unsatisfied, and the manager lost out on a £60 sale, thinking I was just another browser.

I think we've all said, at some time or another, 'I wish I'd bought that.' The next time you say it, recognize it as a sign of a salesperson not having closed a sale.

And that, in a tiny nutshell, is the sales process. Very simple yet at the same time very challenging to execute well. Unfortunately, the process of selling is too often perceived as (and taught to be) a game in which the objective is to get as much money from the customer as possible. This idea is distasteful to most of us and explains the negative images we associate with 'salespeople'.

Selling should be a process by which salespeople do everything in their power to ensure that customers have their needs fulfilled. It is not a game, and there should be no losers. Effective selling always leads to a win-win conclusion, in which you and your customer each finish the sales interview a little better off than when you began. Your customer leaves without the burden of an unsatisfied need, and you leave with fair financial reimbursement.

Skipping any one of the steps in the sales process will not lead to a win-win conclusion. In fact, missing a step can, and often does, set the stage for potential conflict.

Function 2: A service person makes customers comfortable

The second function of the salesperson is to make customers comfortable. You want your customers to be relaxed, to feel at home and at ease, as if they are among friends.

I don't think many of us really ever go out of our way to make a customer feel uncomfortable. Yet most of us have made at least one of the classic mistakes that ends in that result. Sometimes we chat to our friends or colleagues when customers are around, making them feel like intruders. Sometimes we spout off rules and regulations that make our customers feel uncomfortable. Sometimes we badger and hound our customers. And, worst of all, sometimes we just ignore them.

Making customers comfortable is easy to talk about but not always easy to do. The challenge is that, to achieve a significant level of comfort for our customers, we often must sacrifice some of our own comfort.

'How many of you', I have asked in my retail seminars, 'really and truly care about your customers' comfort?' Usually, around 90 per cent of the hands in the room go up.

'OK', I continue. 'Now all of you who have ever started pulling the doors partway closed 5 or 10 minutes early put your hands down.' About a third of the hands go down.

'Now put your hands down if you have ever chatted to friends or colleagues while there were customers in the shop.' Down go another several hands.

'Does anyone here start balancing the cash, only to have a customer show up? Does anyone vacuum when the shop is open? Does anyone chew gum while talking to customers?' By this time, few, if any, hands remain in the air.

Customer comfort means speaking more slowly on the telephone. It means sometimes staying past closing time. It means asking your friends not to drop by or telephone when you're working. It means not smoking around customers. It means changing your routine to include some activities with which you may not now be comfortable.

Part of ensuring a customer's comfort is being aware of your own verbal skills and body language. As we will cover in Chapter 6, 'Listening to your customer', the way you say things plays a huge role in how your customers behave. Even when your mouth's not talking, your body is, and it may not be sending the messages you intend. Do you cross your arms when you're talking to customers? Do you avoid eye contact? Do you slouch? If you do any of these things, you're saying 'I'm unreceptive, and I don't particularly care very much.'

Do you always smile? (Note that I use the word 'always'. I'm not asking if you smile 60 per cent of the time, or 70 or 80 per cent of the time, but if you always smile when the customer is there.) We all know that smiling is important, and most of us think we smile, but a quick look at any service situation will show you how few people really do. Smiling is critical in customer service; if you're not prepared to smile, then you'd best be prepared for grumpy customers. It doesn't count if you're smiling inside or even if you're smiling with your eyes. Smiling is a way of telling your customers that you care and that you want them to be comfortable in your shop.

Function 3: A service person is an ambassador for the company

The third function of a service person is to represent the company. Sometimes we forget that, even when we're not wearing the company uniform, not driving in the company car or not working on the sales floor, we are still ambassadors for our company. We often, all too publicly, say negative things about our companies, managers and work environments without fully understanding the impacts of doing so on our customers and sales.

In fact, the indirect influence we have on the success of our businesses is far greater than we realize. We all have friends and family who are loyal to us and to whom we are loyal. They patronize our companies, and encourage others to do so, because we work there. We do the same for them.

For 24 years, my brother worked as the information systems manager in the head office of a grocery chain. In those 24 years, he ate and drank and slept this company. He wore all of the company's promotional clothing. Many of the birthday and Christmas presents he and his wife gave people had the company's name stamped on them. And we all knew that, if he came by for a visit and saw a bag from a competitor lying around, we'd be in deep trouble indeed. He was the quintessential company man.

Think about this for a moment. How much revenue do you suppose my brother indirectly contributed to his company? It would be impossible to say for sure – I don't know if his sphere of influence is 30 people or 300 people – but I do know for a fact that over the years my family alone purchased more than £10,000 worth of groceries from that company purely out of loyalty to my brother.

An experience I had a while back with the executive of a large international restaurant chain stands in sharp contrast to the loyalty displayed by my brother. We had a lunch appointment. 'Anywhere but one of our restaurants', he told me when asked if he had a preference of where to eat. 'I hate our stuff.' I almost choked. Honest though he might have been, he was doing more damage to his company than he knew. Not only was he biting the hand that fed him, but he was also positioning his company as inferior to its competitors. How's that for setting himself up for potential future problems?

Always remember that, every time you say something negative about your place of business, you are damaging your own credibility as well. Don't ever forget that people expect you to be an ambassador for your company.

Function 4: A service person is always positive

The fourth function of a service person, which is closely related to the third, is always to be positive. How many times have you encountered service people who speak negatively about themselves, the products, their companies or, even worse, their customers? Do you remember the effect these people's attitudes had on your desire to do business with their companies? It's not always easy to be positive, I realize, but if there is one universal truth it's that nobody likes a whiner. It doesn't matter at all how you perceive yourself. If customers perceive you as negative, then you will have conflict.

Often the way customers perceive you has far less to do with what you say than with the way you say it. You really have to be aware of how you choose to phrase things. Imagine that you've just sat down for a drink at the local bar. The barman comes up and says 'What would you like?' You ask for a pint of your favourite ale, to which he replies 'We don't stock it. You'll have to drink something else.'

Now, technically, the barman did nothing wrong. After all, he didn't carry your brand. But did he make you feel comfortable? No. Did he make you feel like you were being a bit of a pain in the backside? Yes. And while this situation alone might not have resulted in conflict, the sense of discomfort might easily have contributed to conflict later on – all because the barman used negative language.

How could he have said it better? Well, how about something like this: 'Good choice. Unfortunately, we're all out at the moment. What other brand can I interest you in?' By choosing his words carefully, he could have made you feel comfortable and welcome and probably won himself a repeat customer.

There are a few words and phrases, negative language, that we hear a lot. The biggest offender is 'You'll have to'. 'You'll have to' is everywhere, and we've all heard it. See if you don't recognize some of the following:

> *In a restaurant:* 'You'll have to wait 20 minutes for a table.'
> Returning merchandise: 'You'll have to show me the receipt.'
> *For a special order:* 'You'll have to leave a deposit.'
> At an airline ticket counter: 'You'll have to tuck the strap of your suitcase in.'
> *In a busy shop:* 'You'll have to wait until I'm finished with this customer.'
> Writing a cheque: 'You'll have to show me two pieces of ID.'

Make a note to yourself. Customers don't have to do anything! Here's how the same sentences might be better expressed:

> *In a restaurant:* 'We'll have a table ready for you in about 20 minutes.'
> Returning merchandise: 'Do you have your receipt?'
> *For a special order:* 'We're all set, and the deposit will be £10.'
> At an airline ticket counter: 'Could I get you to tuck in the strap of your suitcase?'
> *In a busy shop:* 'I'll be with you just as soon as I'm finished with this customer.'
> Writing a cheque: 'Do you have a driving licence and perhaps a major credit card I can look at?'

There are many other forms of negative language, but I'm sure you get the idea. Don't believe, however, that negative language is used only by negative people. Listen to yourself. It's something we're all guilty of from time to time.

In addition to using negative language, we are also often guilty of unintentionally presenting positive things in a negative light. I'll never forget the time I was searching for a fax machine. I was looking at plain-paper machines, and when I asked how much they were the salesperson replied 'They're pretty expensive. About £350.' Why did she say 'They're pretty expensive'? Why didn't she just say 'They're about £350'? Did she think I was cheap? Was she worried that I would complain about the price? I don't know. All I know is that the message I, the customer, received was this: 'I don't think this is good value.' And I'm not sure I want to shop in a shop that doesn't provide good value.

A good salesperson thinks before speaking. You should always ask yourself two questions – 'What is the impact this will have on my customer?' 'Is there a better, more positive way to say it?' – before you open your mouth. Remember: it's not what you say but how you say it.

Function 5: A service person is always honest

The fifth responsibility of a service person is to be honest, to have integrity. Trustworthiness is the hallmark of excellent service people and their companies.

For the most part, in today's business environment, honesty with customers is part of our culture. But many fine service people are now suffering from the effects of a time when making the sale seemed to come before all else. Telemarketers, carpet cleaners and used-car salespeople, to name only a few, often find customers questioning their sincerity and credibility.

You see, the philosophy not all that long ago was that you should never admit to any of your products' shortcomings, never question a customer's choice and never do or say anything that might stand in the way of a sale. This mentality might have been considered good policy for short-term business, but it has haunted salespeople ever since. As a rule of thumb, honesty means never promising what you can't deliver, never promising that a product will deliver what it cannot and never promising that you will stand behind a product if you won't. Honesty, however, does not mean being insensitive. It is usually a good idea to temper your honesty with a little tact. If, for example, you work in a clothing shop and someone comes out of the changing room wearing something that looks terrible on him or her, don't say 'Well, that looks terrible on you!' Try saying something more gentle, such as 'You know, we've got some other styles that I think may be more appropriate.' The rule is to be honest, not brutal.

Function 6: A service person cares

I've left the most important function of the service person to the end. Without this one thing, no company could ever survive: a service person has to care. Genuinely care about the customers. Genuinely care that customers are leaving with something they need. Genuinely care that customers have a problem that needs to be solved. Genuinely care that customers are always comfortable.

Of all the employees I ever hired, perhaps the most impressive salesperson I had the pleasure of working with was a young lady named Beth. Now, Beth would die a thousand deaths if she knew I was referring to her in this book as a 'sales-person'. She hated the label. To her, the word 'salesperson' dredged up images of the parasitic vacuum cleaner salesman with a foot firmly wedged in the door or the used-car salesman who hasn't made a sale in two months. But while Beth didn't have sophisticated selling skills, she was in fact a salesperson – and an excellent one.

What Beth lacked in the technical aspects of selling she made up for with an overwhelming sense of caring for her customers. She cared deeply about making sure that her customers left with exactly what they needed. She was always concerned that perhaps she'd missed something or forgotten something. She never knew it, but the rest of us did – Beth was the soul of that shop. When she left to go to college, the shop's sales dropped, and I don't think it was a coincidence. The last I heard from her, she was teaching somewhere in Costa Rica. I often wonder if the parents of the children she's teaching appreciate what they've got.

We would all do well to take a page from Beth's book. Remember that 8 out of 10 customers who defect from your business, never to come back, leave because they thought you didn't care. They felt unappreciated. It's easy to say that you should care about your customer, but it's not so easy to do. It's difficult to care about everybody when you may have tens of thousands of customers every year. The only way to do it is to take your customers one at a time, deal with them one at a time and care about them one at a time.

It is important that we talk in this book about the service person's job – your job – because any time you are in conflict you are half of the equation. Before we start pointing our fingers at our customers, we want to make sure that the fingers shouldn't be pointed at us. In other words, before you start accusing your customers of being Customers from Hell, you have to ask yourself if you did your job properly. Did you follow all of the steps of the sales process? Was your customer comfortable the whole way through? Were you an ambassador for your company? Were you always honest with your customer? Were you always positive? If someone wanted to pay by cheque, did you say 'We'd be delighted to take your cheque. Do you have a driving licence I could take a look at and perhaps a major credit card?' Or did you say 'Yes, we can take a cheque. But you'll need two pieces of ID'? The difference in language is subtle, but the difference in effect is dramatic. And, finally, did you really care? This is an important self-evaluation process to go through, because often those Customers from Hell aren't Customers from Hell at all. Sometimes the fault is with us. Yes, even you.

A 'difficult customer' is very much in the eye of the beholder. For instance, you may perceive someone to whom you are having difficulty making a sale as a difficult customer. But the problem may actually be with your own skill level. I remember being stranded on the side of the road once with a flat tyre. I had the car jacked up and was hopelessly struggling to remove the rusted wheel nuts from the rim. I had spent 20 minutes on the stupid thing when a mechanic finally happened by. With three squirts of rust remover and a deft, sharp twist, the rim was off. It turned out that the tyre wasn't difficult at all… at least not for a person who knew what to do.

'I had a customer yesterday,' Susan, a pharmaceutical call centre employee once told me in earnest, 'who insisted on asking me question after question about this product. She wanted to know about side-effects and compatibility with everything from aspirin to ice cream. She had me on the phone for 45 minutes. Meanwhile, the waiting time for the queue had grown to over 10 minutes, and other callers were starting to get upset. I probably get people like that once a week, and they drive me mad.'

To Susan, this was a Customer from Hell. To me, it was a service person who, although quite motivated, maybe wasn't doing her job as well as she could have. I took the opportunity to ask her a few questions.

'Had she ever taken the drug before?'

'I don't know', Susan replied.

I then asked 'How often does she get side effects from other drugs?'

'I don't know', she said again.

'What had she heard about the drug and from whom?' I persisted.

'I don't know', said Susan, beginning to get exasperated with me. 'She didn't tell me any of these things.'

'Did you ask her any of these things?'

She paused for a moment and looked at me. 'No', she said finally.

Here was a situation in which the customer had taken complete control and had done so because Susan, the service person, had not taken control. The service person had made no attempt to determine what the customer's real concerns were, and the customer, who lacked knowledge of the drug, was attempting to satisfy her concerns by trial and error.

I explained to Susan that, had she taken the time to discover the woman's needs by asking her some probing questions, there was a chance that the conversation might have been successfully conducted in considerably less time. Susan's questions should have been about why the customer was concerned, what experiences she'd had in the past, what her doctor had told her, what the pharmacist had told her and so on.

Susan nodded at me, looking somewhat unconvinced. But she agreed that the next time she came across one of these customers she would do as I had suggested and see how it worked.

The next week I was back at the call centre, and she came up to me. 'It worked!' she said excitedly. 'What you said worked. I had two of them just this week. I did exactly what you said, and I was off the phone with them in under five minutes. One of them even commented on how wonderful I was!'

To me, a customer who requires some extra effort is not a difficult customer. As our level of selling skill increases, the challenge presented by these customers decreases.

Am I expecting too much from someone who is 'just a service person'? I don't think so. I strongly believe, and have told anybody who will listen, that customer service jobs today are among the most difficult occupations out there. The skill sets required to survive and excel are numerous and diverse. The number of customers with whom we come into contact can be staggering. The training we receive is often minimal (or non-existent), yet the expectations our customers have of us are high. Customer service may very well be the most undervalued occupation on the planet.

4

Controlling your emotions

The greater the emotional aspect of a conflict, the more intense the level of confrontation. The more intense the level of confrontation, the more difficult the situation is to resolve.

It's all well and good to understand the theory of conflict, but it's another thing altogether to put it to use. We all know what really happens. Suddenly, the Customer from Hell is in our face. The customer is belligerent, or swearing, or lying, or trying to negotiate with us. The customer may be abusive, whining, impatient or just plain loud. The customer is all of the things that drive us mad. Our initial response to this kind of behaviour is neither intellectual nor logical. It's instinctive. It comes from the gut. I'm quite sure that I don't know anyone who could just sit back, listen to this kind of assault and calmly ponder the theory of conflict. 'OK, let's see here. This person 2 inches from my face, screaming at me, has come in with a need, a situation and a circumstance, coupled with a specific personality and predisposition. This has created a motivating set of expectations within the customer. Now how should I deal with this?'

It would be wonderful if we all had the capacity to be so dispassionate, but, as *Star Trek*'s Mr Spock puts it, 'Humans are quite emotional, aren't they?' I think we all recognize the signs of emotion within us. Some of us feel the hair on the backs of our necks starting to bristle. A sinking sensation in the stomach. A tingly feeling inside. Your head may start to feel warmer. Your breath may come a little faster. Your heart rate may go up. Adrenalin begins coursing through the body as physiological defence mechanisms start to kick in. Fight or flight. This is the turning point for conflict. It is the point at which conflict can become confrontation.

Confrontation is a result of conflicting emotional states between two people. These emotional states must be addressed before the confrontation can be prevented or resolved. The greater the emotional aspect of a conflict, the more intense the level of confrontation. The more intense the level of confrontation, the more difficult the situation is to resolve. So, regardless of the customer, regardless of the behaviour the customer is manifesting, regardless of the situation, the critical first step you must take is to minimize the possibility and extent of confrontation.

There are really only three basic elements in managing any difficult situation:

▥ managing your personal emotional state;
▥ managing the other person's emotional state; and
▥ solving the problem.

The first two elements will help you to minimize the intensity and duration of any confrontation. The third element, solving the problem, is the intellectual part and, believe it or not, is the easiest part of the process. This chapter focuses on strategies for the first element: managing your personal emotional state. It is essential that you master this if you hope to master conflict resolution.

Let's examine what happens in the first few seconds of a difficult situation. Think for a moment about the way you typically respond to crisis, stress or conflict. Do you get angry and shout? Do you cry? Do you whine? Do you walk away? Do you cower to avoid the situation? Do you sulk? Do you snipe or take pot-shots at the other person? We all react instinctively, and chances are that you, like the rest of us, do not respond well. But can your reaction be controlled? Is it learnt behaviour, or is it something we were born with?

These are all behavioural responses that we have learnt and perfected throughout our lifetimes and that consequently we have the ability to change. When we talk about managing emotions, what we are really talking about is managing the emotional state, the behaviour, the responses to our emotions. It would be a mistake to believe that it is somehow a good thing for us to try to subvert or suppress our emotions or pretend that they aren't there. That just doesn't work. Emotions such as fear, frustration, anxiety, happiness, joy and love are all very real. They are part of the human make-up. But the ways that we respond to these emotions – with anger, rage, insecurity, sullenness, laughter and so on – are all very controllable. You'll see that there are different ways to manage them.

How we react to our emotions is patterned behaviour. Our emotional states, and consequently our behaviours, are determined by specific triggers. The moment one of our 'buttons' is pushed, the corresponding emotion is triggered, and our predetermined behaviour pattern begins. Anthony Robbins, one of today's truly brilliant motivational speakers, perhaps describes the process the best. He uses the metaphor of a record playing in one's mind. (Remember records? Kind of like big CDs with holes in the middle.) When an emotional response is triggered, it is very much like a needle falling down on a record. The same old song starts to play, and it plays right through to the end.

The trigger can be something quite innocuous, such as a harmless joke or an unintentional reproach – someone says 'Your mother dresses you funny' or 'Haven't you worked this out yet?' But to you it may well represent a lack of respect, a criticism or a scolding. The behavioural pattern that results from this trigger, the same old song that our record plays, depends on how we have learnt to respond over the years.

As children, we may have learnt to get our way in a stressful situation by yelling and screaming and carrying on until people eventually backed down. Or we learnt that if we cried people would eventually feel sorry for us and give us what we wanted. If we whined, people would give up in frustration. By just remaining sullen, we could make other people feel guilty.

Changing these responses perhaps isn't as difficult as it may first appear. It really involves only two things: learning to recognize the triggers that get you started and then disrupting the pattern, or 'scratching' the record, before you get too far into the song.

Our emotional triggers

We all have emotional triggers. Some of us have more than others, and they are different for each of us. Have you ever noticed, for example, how you can say one thing to one person and that person will just laugh it off, yet saying the same thing to somebody else will trigger a full-scale explosion?

A friend of mine is a lawyer, and you can imagine how much abuse he puts up with under the guise of lawyer jokes. He laughs with the best of us and even manages to tell a few of his own. I met a lawyer recently, however, for whom these jokes are no laughing matter. When somebody makes the mistake of telling a lawyer joke around him, he not only does not laugh, but also launches into an angry monologue on the inappropriateness of this 'humour'.

The issue here isn't which one of these two lawyers has the right attitude. The issue is that for one of them lawyer jokes are a trigger that sets off an emotional response. I make this point because we often ask ourselves why people are reacting in unexpected ways. 'Why are they acting so unreasonably?' we wonder. Different people do react differently, but it doesn't necessarily mean they are being unreasonable. Just because somebody responds differently to you doesn't mean that person is being unreasonable.

Identifying your triggers

Grab a piece of paper and a pen. If you don't have them handy, set the book down and go and get them. Now take a few minutes to think about what sets you off. Criticism? Threats? A lack of respect? Swearing? Suppression of your creativity? Somebody not listening to your point of view? People who speak loudly? There are as many different triggers as there are people. What are yours? Give some thought to this exercise. Give some real thought to it. Think about the last time you got angry. What was it that got you going? What was it that the other person said or did or didn't say or do? Write down your triggers. Beside each one, write down why you think it affects you. What is it about your personality that has created these triggers?

This is a very difficult self-analysis project, but it is also a very important first step. It is unrealistic to expect that you can manage your emotional state if you don't have some idea of what it is that creates that state. One of the amazing things about the human brain and human psychology is that we can begin to master our emotional states simply by identifying what our triggers are. We can begin to rationalize what was once just an automatic response.

Breaking the pattern

Emotional states are progressive. Except in the rarest of situations, we don't instantly switch from being contented to being angry or sad. From the initial trigger that sets us off, our emotions continue to build gradually within us, fuelled by our racing thoughts and our past experiences. And in confrontational situations, it's not just a matter of one person struggling with an ever-increasing emotional state. It's two or more people feeding off each other, creating even greater tension and anxiety.

Once I was flying back from Disneyworld with my wife, our three children and my brother and sister-in-law. The first leg of our flight had been delayed, which created a problem with our connection. We ran to the gate, only to discover that we had been given the wrong gate number. By the time we arrived at the right gate, our seats had been given to other passengers, and we were informed that we'd been moved to the next flight. That was, of course, if they could get us on the next flight, which was also overbooked.

The attendant at the gate was clearly having a stressful day. It was obvious that we weren't the first people to whom she'd had to break bad news. I, too, was under some stress. After we arrived at our home airport, I still had to make a five-hour drive to get to another town for an 8 am seminar the next morning. The confrontation started with three words: 'We've been moved?' I asked incredulously.

That was all it took for the gate attendant, who turned to me with fire in her eyes. 'This wouldn't have happened if you had been here on time, sir!' came the scold.

You can imagine the effect that had on me. I tersely explained my situation and emphasized the fact that a foul-up on the part of her airline had caused us to be late. I then upped the emotional ante a little and suggested to her that the oversold seating was the airline's problem, not mine.

This, of course, pushed a couple of her own buttons. It was now her turn to crank up the heat a bit. Her voice got a little louder, she looked me in the eye and she stated firmly, 'No, sir, it is very much your problem. You are not on the aeroplane!'

My blood pressure went off the scale. I was ready for a fight, and she was going to be on the losing end. By the time this thing was through, I was determined to have seats on that aeroplane and her job.

Fortunately, I never got the chance to really work myself into a tizzy. My brother, who wasn't facing the same kind of time restraints I was, calmly stepped in and masterfully resolved the situation to everyone's benefit. With 40 years of sibling experience behind him, he was able to recognize my emotional state and knew that things were only going to get worse.

What he did, essentially, was interrupt the emotional pattern he saw developing. He took the 'I'm really mad, and I'm going to get you' record that had started to play in my mind and scratched it. He removed me from the situation just long enough for the emotional edge to disappear and the logical part of my brain to kick in.

Unfortunately, when we're faced with an emotional situation at work, we don't usually have a third party to rescue us. We're left to our own devices to change our own emotional states. That's why it is so important that we learn to understand the triggers that get us going, because the next step to controlling our emotional states is to start disrupting the learnt behavioural patterns that follow. That is, you must find something you can do yourself that will scratch the record playing in your brain, something that will interrupt the usual progression of emotions and behaviour.

To do this, you must learn to redirect your focus sharply. You must learn to give different meanings to the buttons that have been pushed in you so that they can be replaced by new, more productive responses. If, for example, you begin to feel defensive and start to get angry when someone says 'You don't know what you're talking about', you need to change that response to one that brings you confidence. If a person who shouts or uses foul language intimidates you, you need to change your reaction, perhaps to one of sympathy for someone who has poor interpersonal skills. In my case, the message I got from the airline person was 'Who cares if you're the customer?' If I had tried, I could have turned my outrage into empathy by imagining the stress that gate attendant must have been under.

There are many different ways to break your initial emotional pattern. We've all seen the old routine in the movies where someone slaps a hysterical person in the face and that person responds 'Thanks, I needed that!' As clichéd as it seems, this is actually a classic pattern interrupter. It shifts the person's focus from the problem to a stinging cheek, and this instantly begins to generate a series of internal questions. What? Why did the person do that? What do I do now? As the focus changes, so does the person's behaviour.

Another classic pattern interrupter is the one recommended for people who become terrified at having to speak in public. You know, the old 'Picture everyone in the audience in their underwear' trick. Silly as it sounds, it works for many people. But why does this underwear thing work?

Think about the last time you had to give a speech. If you were nervous, the one big thought running through your mind was 'Oh, God, I hope I don't screw up.' The next thing you know, you're standing in front of the audience, shaking like a leaf. You're self-conscious and acutely aware of everything you say and how you say it. To your horror, you realize that you have tripped over a word or inadvertently missed part of your speech. Chances are your audience didn't notice, but you did, and your anxiety is now even greater. This increased anxiety causes you to make another error, which increases your anxiety even more, creating more errors, and so on. You're locked into a classic 'anxiety–error–anxiety' spiral.

The 'picturing people in their underwear' technique helps to break that spiral by briefly (and dramatically) shifting your concentration away from your own fears to your audience, long enough to give you a running start in the right direction. In theory, it allows you the opportunity to push the spiral upward instead of downward.

Think about the same process in terms of dealing with the Customer from Hell. The negative cycle may begin with someone at the counter shouting 'I've been waiting for 20 minutes! Why does it take you so long to do a simple price check?' The salesperson gets defensive and responds with a gentle scold: 'I can't do anything about it. It's a big shop, you know.' This response irritates the customer even more, thus escalating the confrontation.

What if, in this situation, the salesperson visualized the customer standing there in underwear? Would the reaction have been quite as defensive? I don't think so. It's hard to feel threatened by people who shop in their underwear. I'm not suggesting, of course, that we shouldn't take our customers seriously. We should. It's just really important that we find ways to begin responding differently to their unpleasant behaviours.

Pattern-interruption techniques can be quite effective, but when the person is only a foot or two away from you and in your face you may need to think of something a little more graphic. Instead of picturing your Customer from Hell standing there in underwear, picture him or her standing there in a nappy. In your mind, stick a gigantic dummy in his or her mouth. Put a huge blue beehive like Marge Simpson's on the top of the customer's head with a gigantic pink ribbon on top. Give female tormentors moustaches and male tormentors bras. You want something that is graphic enough, silly enough and mad enough to direct your focus away from your own needs and your own emotions, very much like a figurative slap in the face.

Of course, not all of us have the ability to visualize. But you can achieve the same pattern-interrupting result with a slight variation on the same technique. When I'm conducting workshops, I hand every participant a couple of blank sheets of paper and a box of crayons. The instructions are simple: draw a picture of the Customer from Hell. Make the most ridiculous, most fearsome customer you can imagine. Draw two mouths. Have red smoke coming out of the customer's nose and green stuff oozing from the ears. There is only one rule: you have to use every colour of crayon in the box to make the picture. I can tell you, I've had many a Serious Service Person give me some pretty strange looks during this segment of the workshop.

Just for fun, put down this book again, grab another piece of paper and some crayons or coloured markers, and try it yourself. Oh, I know you'll feel silly, but try it anyway. If nothing else, you'll get to relive your childhood for a few moments. Once you've completed your picture, write the name 'Lester' under it. The reason for the name will become apparent as you read on in this book. If you just can't bring yourself to draw a picture, run down to the local shopping centre and use one of those mini photo booths. Make weird faces. Make a rude hand gesture. Do something that's memorable. Give yourself something visual to work with. Now put Lester somewhere easily accessible (under a counter, in a desk drawer, in your briefcase). If you're in a call centre, you can tape it to the wall in front of you.

As soon as you realize you've come into contact with a difficult customer, as soon as you realize that your buttons are being pushed, as soon as you feel your emotions starting to swell, take a quick peek at your picture of Lester. Then take a look at your customer. This may not appear to be a very sophisticated method of controlling your emotions, but I challenge you to do this exercise without experiencing a fairly significant shift in emotional state. Just a word of warning, however: laughing out loud or showing the picture to your customer is not recommended.

Here's another method. On yet another piece of paper, write down one word or phrase. It can be any word or phrase you like, but it has to be unusual, one you don't use regularly. Again, the way to apply it is simple: when you are faced with that special customer, say that word in your mind (not out loud!) before you even open your mouth.

There are lots of other ways to interrupt your emotional state, but these two are good ones. What you are trying to achieve, again, is brief but dramatic change to mental focus.

Keeping it broken

These pattern-interruption techniques momentarily slow your behavioural pattern, which is the important first step. But what you really want to do is eliminate emotion from the equation and change the trigger permanently. You ultimately want to get to the stage where specific customer behaviour no longer lights your fuse. You do so by learning to ask yourself focusing questions.

Suppose you've just encountered a Customer from Hell who has suggested to you that you're lazy, which happens to be something that makes you angry. You've used your picture of

Lester and momentarily gained control of your emotional state. What we typically do at this stage is start asking ourselves questions: 'Who does he think he is, calling me lazy?' or 'What can I do to prove to her that she's wrong?' Unfortunately, these questions don't solve anything; in fact, these are the questions that make us angrier and add fuel to the fire.

What you need to do now is pose a whole new set of questions: 'Why is this customer so agitated?' 'What's the real issue here?' 'How am I going to resolve this problem?' Asking such questions begins the process of focusing your thoughts on the issue instead of the emotions.

Under your picture of Lester, write three focusing questions:

▪ Why is this customer so agitated?
▪ What is the real issue?
▪ How can we resolve this?

These are questions to ask *yourself*, of course, not your customer. Be aware that the answers to these questions are not always easily found. Although an answer may seem pretty obvious at times (eg 'He needs to return something that didn't work properly'), remember the five elements of expectations: need, situation, circumstance, personality and predisposition. There is almost always more going on than is immediately obvious, and it requires a great deal of skill and more than a little patience to identify the whole reason for a customer's behaviour. If you truly concentrate on seeking the answers to these questions, if you make a real effort to understand your customer better, you'll be pleasantly surprised at the productive, constructive manner in which you will begin to approach problems.

For pattern interrupters and focusing questions truly to work, you have to make them work. You have to be committed to making them work. You have to learn to want to resolve the conflict. If you take the 'What an idiot – I'll teach him for talking to me like that' attitude, then you might as well not even bother trying a pattern interrupter, because it won't work. If your focusing questions are negative – 'What's this idiot's problem?' 'What kind of personality disorder does she have?' 'How can I shut him up?' – you will resolve nothing. The successful approach to the challenge of conflict always involves asking yourself 'How do we make this work to everyone's benefit?' instead of asking 'How can I win?'

Since you've already got that pen and paper handy, I'm going to ask you to do something else. Take a few moments to write down some specific instances when you encountered a Customer from Hell. Try to record as many instances as you can. Put down as much detail as you can remember. Now take a look at that list and see if there are any similarities or trends. Do there tend to be any similar circumstances or situations involved? Does the conflict often involve a particular type of customer need? Are there specific (apparent) personality types involved when you find yourself in conflict? Do similar apparent predispositions appear to be present? If you spot any trends, write them down below your list. Make a commitment to yourself that the next time you find yourself in a similar situation you will make a conscious effort to break your emotional pattern and ask yourself the three focusing questions.

All right now. You've come face to face with a Customer from Hell, successfully interrupted your emotional pattern and asked yourself the focusing questions. It now becomes important that you maintain this little bit of control and keep yourself from starting to play that emotional record again. You need to concentrate and apply the techniques in the following chapter as well as demonstrate a genuine desire to resolve the situation before it gets ugly.

The good news

Here's the good news. After you've successfully used a pattern interrupter and the focusing questions over a period of time, you'll find yourself consciously using the techniques less and less often. Eventually, your brain will eliminate the techniques, and the trigger that used to set off a reactive emotional response will now automatically set off the questioning process. You will have begun to change your approach to conflict from a fight-or-flight response to a constructive resolution process.

Six months after I conducted a seminar on managing difficult situations, I received a letter from a receptionist with an admittedly short fuse. She wrote to me to proclaim proudly that she hadn't had to look at her (very graphic) picture of Lester in more than two months and that she no longer 'lost it' when a Customer from Hell popped by for a visit. 'Now I just look at my Lester picture when I'm fighting with my husband!' she said.

5

Introducing LESTER

The nifty part of the whole process is that you don't have to wait for your next Customer from Hell to show up in order to practise it.

LESTER is an acronym for the six steps to resolving the vast majority of difficult situations you will encounter in a retail or any other environment. The steps include:

Listening to your customer.
Echoing the issue.
Sympathizing with your customer's emotional state.
Thanking your customer for his or her input.
Evaluating your options.
Responding with a win–win solution.

This approach, which works better than any other conflict-resolution formula I have so far encountered, is based on one fundamental principle: the vast majority of difficult situations we encounter are the result of people who are unsatisfied, not people who are unreasonable. If we listen well enough to what these people have to say, the solutions to conflicts become much more apparent. LESTER will help you to break quickly through the elements of the situation that appear to be unreasonable and will give you the ability to identify and resolve the causes of the dissatisfaction.

To make LESTER work for you, you must begin by accepting, at least for the time being, that nobody really wakes up in the morning and says 'By God, if I do nothing else today, I'm going to be a pain in the backside to somebody.' You must believe that most people are like you and me. We have needs, our unique circumstances, our background situations, our own personalities and our predispositions, all of which dictate our expectations. LESTER uses specific techniques to help you focus on and identify these expectations and thus deal with customers effectively.

LESTER is an intriguing concept once you've embraced it. As you practise and perfect it, you will begin to find that conflicts at work and at home are far less stressful. You will discover the true sense of satisfaction that comes from resolving conflict instead of contributing to it.

Although I describe LESTER as a six-step process, it need not be either time-consuming or complex. Depending on the severity of the situation, it can be executed successfully in 90 seconds or nine minutes. In fact, the greatest challenge you will face is the same one we face when confronted with any new skill: the temptation to say 'I'm already doing all that!' None of the individual components of LESTER is likely to come as a massive revelation to you. I would suspect you're already using some of the skills, so you may find yourself feeling as if you know all this. But unless you're very different to the rest of us, you're not nearly as consistent, or as good at it, as you think you are.

The next six chapters detail the components of LESTER. If you are truly interested in mastering this process, I would suggest that you try to find some time to practise each component before you move on to the next. Doing this will help you to lock the process in your mind and, as a result, will make it easier to remember when an opportunity to use it arises.

The nifty part of this whole process is that you don't have to wait for your next Customer from Hell to show up in order to practise it. It works at home as well as it does on the job, and it applies to everyday situations as well as conflict situations. And the best part is that learning to master your own emotional states and using the principles outlined in the next few chapters have significant side effects. These skills will also have a dramatic effect on how you are perceived by those customers with whom you are not in conflict.

Let's say, for example, that you have a shop full of people when, out of the blue, a customer gets in your face and starts shouting at you. 'This is ridiculous! You call yourself a jeans shop, but you never have my size in stock. I have asked and asked and asked, but you never get my size in stock. If you ask me, I think this is a pretty shoddy way of doing business!' This customer now has your full attention as well as the attention of every other customer in the store. Like you, the other customers are uncomfortable, and for the most part their instinctive response will be to sympathize with you. Their loyalty will change instantly, however, if you mishandle the situation. So you discreetly usher your customer off to a quiet corner of the store while you gain control of your emotions. You patiently and attentively listen, echoing the customer's points. You sympathize with the customer's position, thank the customer very much for his or her input, determine what can be done and respond to the situation. The customer walks away satisfied, believing that you really do care.

When these situations occur, you will often find that other customers later comment on how well you handled the situation. Many times I have had customers come up to me after I have managed an unpleasant situation and say 'I'm glad I wasn't in your shoes' or 'It takes all kinds, doesn't it?' or 'Isn't that awful? He had no right to talk to you like that.' When dealing with difficult situations, you must always be aware of the comfort level of the other customers around you. The time may come when you have to shift your focus from the needs of the Customer from Hell to the needs of the other customers.

6

Listening to your customer

The most common and most devastating mistake people make when faced with a Customer from Hell is to try to resolve the problem before really understanding what the problem is.

Listening. Sounds pretty basic so far, doesn't it? After all, you're a good listener, aren't you? This chapter should be a breeze. Well, before you skim through it and move on, let's talk about what listening really is.

First of all, as you are no doubt aware, there is a dramatic difference between listening and hearing. Hearing is physiological. Hearing is the body's response to sound waves. Listening, on the other hand, is the translation of these sound waves into meaning in the brain. Most of us can hear. Most of us can listen. But it is how we listen that makes the difference between good listeners and poor listeners.

Listening is broken down by most experts into four levels. Without burdening you with a lot of detail, I can explain that someone who is listening at level four is simply not paying attention. The words are going in one ear and, as they say, out the other. Level-one listeners, on the other hand, have trained themselves to listen. Level-one listeners miss nothing. They

understand and appreciate all that they hear. Most of us fluc-
tuate between level-two and level-three listening, which usually
provides us with adequate information to complete our day-to-
day tasks.

Have you ever been in the middle of a conversation with
somebody and discovered to your horror that you haven't
heard a word the person has said for the past 15 seconds – and,
even worse, that the person is awaiting your reply to some deep
question? Or have you ever had a long conversation with
somebody and discovered afterwards that the two of you were
talking about two completely different things? Has anybody
ever said to you 'That's not what I meant'? Has anybody ever
said to you 'I just said that'? These are signs that we're not
listening to the best of our capabilities, and it happens to all of
us at some time or another. But there are good reasons for this:
we are not born level-one listeners, and level-one listeners are
not level-one listeners all the time.

Try this simple game with a friend. Go to a new restaurant or
some other unfamiliar place. Give your friend 10 seconds to
look around the room and memorize everything he or she can
see that is white. Then ask the friend to close his or her eyes and
name everything in the room that is green. The friend will recall
very little if anything. It's a tremendous demonstration that we
have the capacity to remember and make meaningful only those
things on which we focus.

Think for a moment about the implications if we were able to
concentrate completely on everything that we see or hear.
Imagine what it would be like to be able to recall at a moment's
notice the tiniest detail. Take a look around you. How many
different things can you see in the room you are sitting in now?
The textures, the colours. What sounds can you hear at this
moment? Now imagine if every little thing became committed
to memory!

To compensate for this information overload, our brains
have been bestowed with a fairly complex filtering system. As
information comes in through any of the five senses, your brain
makes an instantaneous decision about whether to capture that

information or let it go by. It then stores the selected information in your short-term memory and later on stores certain items in your long-term memory. What's interesting is that each of us has a unique set of filters. Have you ever noticed that some people can remember things you can't recall? Have you ever wondered how it is that somebody could forget something that you've remembered?

Some people, for example, have the wonderful ability to remember names and faces. And most of us are in awe of that salesperson who can remember the name of a customer who comes in only once a year. Other people have a knack for remembering phone numbers or what other people wear. We all have filters that we've developed over time.

Level-one listeners have trained themselves to remove most of their filters and absorb virtually everything for brief periods of time. This is an important skill because, as we will discover, information is the key to understanding. And the key to getting this kind of information is to improve our listening skills.

Paradigm shifts

Our beliefs and values all originate from the information we receive. As we learn more about people, places and things – in other words, as our information changes – our beliefs and values begin to change accordingly. New information that challenges our beliefs is a part of all of our lives. Think of some of the biggies: the Earth is flat; people aren't meant to fly; the Earth is the centre of the Universe. We've all had to change our opinions at some points in our lives. After a while, the evidence becomes too great to ignore, and we are forced to re-evaluate some fundamental beliefs.

When new information challenges, and ultimately changes, an existing belief, we experience what is called a 'paradigm shift'. A 'paradigm shift' is just a trendy term that simply means a change in the rules or a change in understanding. We experience paradigm shifts throughout our lives. For two days, you curse the manufacturer of your new television set because it hasn't worked all weekend, and then the person who comes to repair it tells you it wasn't plugged in. You brag to your friends about your tough dog, Rambo, and then discover 'he' has given birth to a litter of pups. The person you've always thought of as snooty turns out to be just painfully shy. Paradigm shifts can be mundane, or they can be quite dramatic.

In 1993, I was conducting a motivational customer service seminar for a large group on the West Coast of the United States. I was about an hour into the programme, right in the middle of a segment on the importance of smiling and body language. As you may expect, I like to get quite animated, and I challenge the audience a bit. It's a lot of fun, and everybody has a good laugh. Well, in this seminar, sitting dead centre about five rows back, with her arms crossed and the biggest frown you can imagine, was a middle-aged woman named Jane. She stared and frowned at me to the point that it became unnerving. The unstated message, I thought, was clear: 'I don't want to be here. I think you're stupid. I think the things you're saying are even more stupid. I refuse to laugh or smile, and there's nothing you can do that's going to make me.'

I responded to this, as I do to most challenges, by trying even harder to make her at least smile. It became a mission but was to no avail. The worst part was that I could see the people sitting around her becoming increasingly uncomfortable. This began to make me feel frustrated. 'Can't this woman see the effects she's having on everybody else?' I wondered. 'Can't she see that she's exuding the very behaviour I'm trying to convince people to eliminate?' I had a break shortly after, and I couldn't get her out of my mind.

Apart from my personal frustration, I was concerned about the significant impacts she was beginning to have on the rest of the audience. So I sat down for a few minutes to collect my thoughts and develop a strategy on how to deal with Jane. As I was sitting there, planning my approach, the district supervisor walked up to me with a big smile and said 'It looks like things are going pretty well!'

I smiled back and said 'Yes, they are. Good group. It really is tough to make Jane smile, though.'

The supervisor heaved a big sigh. 'Jane,' he said. 'I can't even believe she's here. Eight days ago her 14-year-old son was killed in a hit-and-run accident as he was walking to a football game. The driver was drunk and ran right off the road on to the pavement. She didn't have to come today, but she thought it might be a good distraction from what she's going through.'

I felt really stupid! My perspective on the situation changed instantly. Do you think I was still feeling frustrated? Quite the opposite, in fact. I was suddenly feeling pity, empathy, sympathy. It is a moment I will never, ever forget. That was a paradigm shift.

Imagine what might have happened had I not had the extreme good fortune to have the supervisor come in and give me that extra bit of information. What do you suppose might have happened had I confronted her? Is it possible that, even if I had been light-hearted and gentle, I would have made the situation worse? I believe it was not only possible but also inevitable.

Have you ever been caught in this kind of situation? Have you ever become angered at something you thought a child, spouse or colleague did and then discovered later that he or she hadn't done it at all? These kinds of paradigm shifts occur often and affect us throughout our lives.

So what's the lesson here? The more information we have before we act, the greater our chances for success and the less likely it is we'll be taken by surprise. This holds true for virtually every aspect of life, and dealing with the Customer from Hell is no different. The more information, the better – and that's what listening is all about.

The principles of listening

There are four fundamental principles of effective listening. As we go through these principles, each one will probably appear to you to be common sense. But as my father used to say, 'The problem with common sense is that it isn't so common.' We are trying to accomplish two things by listening. First, we are trying to get as much information as possible. We need to learn as much as we possibly can about the needs, situations, circumstances, personalities and predispositions that make up our customers' expectations. That, perhaps, is obvious. Second, and perhaps less obvious, we are trying to communicate to our customers (some of whom may very well be agitated) that we do, in fact, care about them and their situations.

Why do we need to communicate that we care? Well, I believe that, if there is one thing that all Customers from Hell have in common, it's that they think you don't care. They think that you (either personally or corporately) are the bad guy. They perceive the interaction as a 'me-versus-you' confrontation. It makes sense to me that, if customers believe that you genuinely care about their problems, they will be a lot more pleasant.

If we've already managed to get some control over our own emotional states, our goal now becomes to try to help our difficult customers gain control over their emotional states. Right now they've got something to get off their chests. Implementing the four principles of effective listening will go a long way to helping you defuse a customer's volatile emotional state.

Principle 1: Undivided attention

The first and most basic principle of listening is to give the other person your undivided attention. What does this mean? Well, it means putting down your clipboard. It means turning to face the person. It means setting aside any other tasks that you are working on. It means not reading your email during the conversation. It means – most importantly – not talking!

Have you ever tried to talk to someone when you weren't quite sure he or she was paying attention? It's a little frustrating, isn't it? You start to get the feeling that the person doesn't really care and that your message isn't getting through. Now put the shoe on the other foot and imagine how that feeling might affect an upset customer. Giving your customers your undivided attention is a critical first step towards communicating to them that you are on their side. Hear them out. Let them know you care.

When you are confronted with an unpleasant situation, it is always a good idea to try, whenever possible, to isolate your customer. If you are on the phone with the customer, make sure that the time is convenient. If you are in a shop, find a quiet, out-of-the-way spot. If you are in a room with other people, ask the customer if he or she would like to find a quieter spot. As well as minimizing the disruption to the rest of the customers and staff, finding a quiet place takes you away from any distractions. It sets you up for success.

Leading customers away from the initial point of confrontation requires a little finesse, however. They may think that you're trying to shuffle them aside or that you are afraid of being embarrassed, and their emotional state will only worsen. Present the move as positive. Let customers know that you believe their concerns are important and that you want to hear them out without any distractions.

For example, instead of saying 'Let's go over here to talk about this', try saying 'This is important to me. Why don't we find a quieter spot so I can give you my undivided attention?' Wording your request this way serves to remove both you and your customer from everyone else and establishes that you consider the person an important customer and that you are interested in what he or she has to say.

Sometimes, of course, customers may insist on staying where they are. If that is the case, you'll have to go with the flow and deal with them on the spot. Whatever you do, don't try to move them again. It will only make things worse.

Principle 2: Eye contact/body language

The second principle of effective listening involves eye contact and body language. There is nothing more unnerving than trying to have a conversation with someone who won't look at you or whose eyes seem to wander during the conversation. Have you ever had a conversation with somebody who is slumped over in a chair, back slightly turned towards you? The message that comes across is loud and clear: 'I don't care, I don't want to be here and I don't really want to be listening to this.' That, of course, may not be the case at all. It is, however, the way we perceive body language.

Many years ago I worked as an account manager in an international advertising agency. One of the most instructive lessons of my early career occurred when a director walked into my office one sunny morning and dropped a videotape on my desk. 'Watch this,' he said, 'and then report to boardroom B at three o'clock.' And with that he turned and strolled out.

I found myself an empty room with a video player, plugged in the tape and sat down. To my great distress, I discovered that the featured topic was me. An hour and a half of me. The executives had set up a camera behind one-way glass in one of the boardrooms and videotaped my meetings and presentations to clients. They had done this with all of my colleagues as well, and the purpose was to prepare us for a training session on presentation skills. The tape was excruciating to watch. My body language was awful: I slouched, I shuffled, my arms flailed and my head bobbed around. It was then that I realized how critical body language is in the communication process.

When you are in a difficult situation with a customer, be very conscious of the subtle yet powerful messages you are sending with your body. Don't cross your arms. If you do, you will be perceived as unreceptive. Don't slouch or lean on something – your customer will think you don't care. Don't cock your hip. If you do, you'll look impatient. Here are some basic rules of body language.

1. Stand up straight

OK, so you heard this a hundred times from your mother – but it's still true. If you slouch, shuffle or keep your head down, you will be perceived as uninterested and ineffective. You simply won't be able to create any kind of connection with your customer.

Keep your arms by your sides or fold your hands (not your arms) in front of you. I suggest you avoid clasping your hands behind your back in the traditional military 'at ease' position. This can come across as 'I'm listening to you not because I want to, but because I have to.'

If you happen to be sitting down, don't lean back. Don't put your feet up or cross your legs. Lean forward and put your forearms on your knees or on the table.

2. Don't square your shoulders to your customer

Be careful about how you stand facing your customer. If your shoulders are square to your customer – that is, so that you are directly face to face – you are in a confrontational position.

The next time you're talking with someone in normal circumstances, take a close look at how you stand. You'll notice that your feet and the feet of the person you are talking to are not directly in front of each other but slightly angled. When you are face to face with an agitated customer, make sure that your stance is similar. Of course, you also want to make sure that you aren't standing at too great an angle. You don't want to give the impression that you would rather be looking somewhere else.

3. Keep your best poker face

In the critical first few moments of a difficult situation, a raised eyebrow, a smile, a frown, even a twitch can be misinterpreted.

4. Stand still

Try not to shift your weight back and forth. Doing so could be perceived as impatience.

5. Look into your customer's eyes

You need to send the message loud and clear that this customer, at this moment in time, is the most important person in your life. I'm not suggesting that you stare at your customer, engaging in a 'who blinks first' contest. But make sure that you are making eye contact, especially when your customer is clearly agitated.

6. Eliminate the barriers

I touched on this when I talked about the importance of giving customers your undivided attention. Barriers such as clipboards, desks and stock stand in the way of creating the atmosphere of trust that is so crucial at this stage. If you are standing behind a counter, move out from behind it. If you are seated at a desk, move so that the desk is no longer between you and your customer. If you are holding a briefcase, put it down.

Such barriers silently reinforce the 'me-versus-them' feelings your customer may already have. To build trust, you must be prepared to create a level of intimacy that encourages your customer to perceive you as a person rather than just a representative of the company.

Our own body language is as difficult to recognize as it is to change, mainly because the ways we move and stand are pure habit. But awareness of our body language in stressful situations can be extremely useful. It's a bit like the pattern-interruption techniques I talked about earlier. The more you focus on your body language, the less you will be able to focus on your emotional state.

Principle 3: Prompt

The third principle of effective listening is prompting. Prompting is the technique we use for encouraging people to continue talking. We all do it to some degree, but for most of us it is a haphazard, instinctive thing. We grunt and mumble at each other to fill the silences, but we don't often give much thought to the real purpose of prompting or how to do it skilfully.

When we have unpleasant situations, we want our customers to talk. We want them to tell us as much as they can. We actively have to encourage them to communicate with us at every opportunity, even if what they are saying is hard to listen to.

The most common and most devastating mistake people make when faced with a Customer from Hell is to try to resolve the problem before really understanding what the problem is. For most of us, our instinctive response when confronted with conflict is to try to remove ourselves from the situation as quickly as possible. Because of this, we more often than not attempt to resolve the conflict before we have adequate information. We respond too quickly.

The results of responding prematurely are never positive, yet in virtually all Customer from Hell encounters that's exactly what we do. Take the following potentially difficult situation as an example:

> *Customer: Do you work here?*
> Salesperson: Yes, sir.
>
> *Customer: Well, I want to know where the hell my widget is, and I want to know now!*
> Salesperson: Which widget is that, sir?
>
> *Customer: The one you people said would be in three weeks ago!*
> Salesperson: May I have your name, sir?
>
> *Customer: Smith. Bob Smith. I've been in here three times, and each time someone tells me 'It should be here in a week.'*
> Salesperson: Let me just check on that, sir. *[Retreats to the back room for a couple of minutes, and then returns.]* It still hasn't arrived, Mr Smith. I'm not sure what the hold-up is, but it should be here any day.
>
> *Customer: [Yelling.] And so should Christmas! I tell you what – you can forget this order! I am sick and tired of this useless company! You don't give a damn about me or my business!*
> Salesperson: Well, we really don't have any control over our suppliers.
>
> *Customer: That's your problem, not mine! Maybe they don't like you either! [Stamps out.]*

Why did the customer walk out? Was it really all the fault of the supplier? Was it just an ill-tempered customer? I don't think so. The seed of discontent perhaps originated with the supplier, and the customer was certainly agitated, but the stressful situation was created by the salesperson's not dealing with the real issue. What was the real issue? Well, let's run the example again, this time a little differently, and find out:

Customer: Do you work here?
Salesperson: Yes, sir.

Customer: Well, I want to know where the hell my widget is, and I want to know now!
Salesperson: Your widget, sir?

Customer: The one you people said would be in three weeks ago!
Salesperson: Oh, no.

Customer: Oh, yes! You people keep telling me 'It should be here in a week', and I've come in three times now!
Salesperson: Really?

Customer: I certainly have. And I tell you it's frustrating. I have to drive 25 miles to get to your shop!
Salesperson: 25 miles?

Customer: [A little more quietly.] I really need this widget.
Salesperson: It certainly sounds like it.

Customer: Well, without it, my new business is never going to get off the ground.
Salesperson: Oh, dear.

Customer: Yes. And the hour and a half of driving back and forth to this shop isn't helping. Every minute I'm out of the office costs me money...

In this example, we've now learnt that, while the problem may be the supplier's tardiness, the issue is the disruption to the customer's business. We're also in a better position to understand why the customer is agitated. We haven't solved the problem yet, but our options for solutions – such as delivery or a direct-from-supplier shipment – are now increasing.

The difference in the second example was that the salesperson prompted the customer with words and phrases such as 'oh no', 'really', 'oh dear', etc. Effective prompting is accomplished with such single words or brief phrases that express interest. It encourages people to talk more, reiterate points and clarify issues.

Effective prompting achieves two crucial objectives. First, it provides you with more information – in this case, we learnt about the new business, the long drive and the financial implications. Second, it gives your customer a chance to wind down and get better control of his emotions.

Perhaps the most common, and unfortunately the least productive, ways of prompting are with the old favourites 'uh-huh' and 'mm-hmm'. When you say 'uh-huh' or 'mm-hmm' to someone, you are sending that person a clear message that you are not terribly interested and that you aren't really paying attention. It's a habit that neither requires nor stimulates thought. Unfortunately, it is also one of the toughest habits in the world to break. But if you can stop grunting at the people you're supposed to be listening to, you'll be amazed at how much your listening will improve.

The practice of prompting is a useful asset not only when dealing with difficult customers, but also in everyday life. The next time you are having a discussion with your spouse, child or colleague, practise this technique. Let the other person do the talking. See how much information you can get with simple words and phrases such as 'oh' and 'really' and 'is that right?'

Here's an example. My 11-year-old daughter came home from school one day to tell me that her teacher had unfairly and undeservedly punished her entire class.

'Really?' I said, trying not to sound incredulous.

'Yes, and we hadn't done anything at all!' my daughter continued.

'Is that right?' I prompted.

'Yes. All we were doing was talking about the assignment, and she just started yelling!'

'Really?'

'I mean' – my daughter looked down a bit – 'she told us yesterday that she didn't want any talking in the class, but we just forgot.'

'You forgot', I said gently.

'Well, I suppose she had a right to be upset, but we didn't do it on purpose.'

Case closed.

What makes prompting so difficult when dealing with unpleasant customers is that they are so, well, unpleasant. We don't really want to listen to any more abuse. It goes against our nature to do anything to encourage unpleasantness. The hidden trap, however, is that, if we fail to prompt, if we fail to extract all the additional and necessary information we can, we risk making unpleasant behaviour worse.

One word of caution with prompting: be very careful about your tone of voice. You want to sound inquisitive and interested, not challenging or sarcastic.

Principle 4: Visualize

The fourth principle of effective listening is to visualize. Try to get a picture in your mind of what the person is saying. Try to understand why the person is feeling the way he or she is. How would you react in that situation if you were in the person's shoes? If you can visualize the expectations of the customer, your understanding of the situation will increase. You will also find that your own emotional state will start to improve. It becomes increasingly difficult to stay upset with somebody when you are standing in that person's shoes.

If you do nothing other than learn to apply these four principles of listening skilfully when difficult situations arise, a curious thing will happen: almost half of these potentially explosive situations will simply evaporate. They will resolve themselves with very little further input on your part. This happens for a few reasons. First, if you have truly spent all that time listening, you haven't had the opportunity to stick your foot in your mouth, to say something that might make the situation worse. (Remember the old saying 'A closed mouth gathers no foot.') Second, if the customer did come in spoiling for a fight, he or she didn't get one. And third, often the complaining customer simply wants to be heard.

Barriers to listening

> *Listen a hundred times. Ponder a thousand times. Speak but once.*
>
> *Turkish proverb*

Shut up!

The barriers to effective listening are many, and most are exceedingly difficult to overcome. Perhaps the greatest one of these is our temptation to talk.

For many of us, the biggest challenge in life is keeping our mouths shut long enough actually to hear what other people are saying. When we're not talking, we're planning what we're going to say next. These habits are developed over a lifetime and are very difficult to break. But break them we must if we want to have any hope of successfully resolving conflict.

Here's a great exercise. The next time you're out at a social function, try not to speak unless you are asked a direct question. Don't be rude, of course. Keep smiling and making eye contact, but just don't talk. Time yourself to see how well you're doing. In addition to being wonderful practice for the next time you're face to face with a Customer from Hell, this exercise will have people around you thinking you're poised, confident and contemplative.

One time I was on a sales call, meeting the director of marketing of a large shopping centre. I introduced myself, allowed myself two or three brief sentences on who we were and what we did, and then said 'So, tell me about the shopping centre!' The meeting lasted almost two hours, and I didn't utter another full sentence. She told me story after story of every marketing programme they had run for the past 20 years. She told me of all the celebrities she had met and of her numerous successes and awards. She told me how she liked to travel three or four times a year. She talked of her children, grandchildren, cousins, nieces and nephews. I knew more about this marketing director by the end of the meeting than I knew about myself. As I was getting up to leave, I offered to send her a reference list of other clients for whom we had worked. She pushed at the air with her hands and said 'I don't need any references! I can tell just from our conversation that you can do the job. Let's plan to start on the 15th of May.' Silence truly is golden.

Be aware of your own stress level

Another great barrier to effective listening is your own stress level. It is tough to devote yourself to other people's problems when you're living with problems of your own. Stresses in business and in your personal life can be distracting at best, and in an often frenzied retail environment the challenge of overcoming them is magnified dramatically.

Be aware of your own emotional state. If you find yourself getting a little overwhelmed, take a short break or even a day off. You're not doing yourself or anyone else any favours by showing up for work when you're not at your best.

I'll say one last thing about improving your skills. Simply reading about listening in this book won't help you. Please don't believe for a second that understanding the concepts alone will make you a better listener. You must practise these skills diligently at home and in non-conflict situations. Practise them at work. Practise them whenever and wherever you can. Make listening a part of your life.

Here again are the basics:

- **Undivided attention.** Drop what you're doing and concentrate on your customer.
- **Eye contact/body language.** Let your customer know you care.
- **Prompt.** Encourage your customer to keep talking.
- **Visualize.** Put yourself in your customer's shoes.

7

Echoing the issue

Let customers have their say, make sure you understand exactly what it is they are saying and let them know you've heard it.

A fascinating thing often happens when we're in a confrontation: we repeat ourselves. We make our points again and again, a little more loudly each time. We reiterate, re-emphasize, restate. We do so because we're convinced that our points aren't getting across, that the other person isn't really listening. 'You just don't get it!' we scream silently.

This is where echoing comes in. Echoing is actually part of the listening process, but I separate it here because it's quite a distinctive skill and one that merits some discussion. Echoing, or reflective listening, is the process by which we feed back to the customer what he or she perceives to be the key issue.

Take this customer in a women's fashion store, for example. 'The salesperson I bought this blouse from three weeks ago promised me that it wouldn't shrink if I washed it in the washing machine', she complains. 'Well, look at it! It must be a whole size smaller! There's no way I can wear it any more. Why don't you people get the information straight on the products you sell?' The salesperson, echoing, would respond with something like 'It's a whole size smaller?'

Echoing is the process of taking a statement made by a customer and repeating the issue back to that customer as close to word for word as possible. This tactic accomplishes three things. First, and most important, it lets customers know that you are, in fact, listening. There will be no need for them to repeat themselves. This helps to reduce the tension and helps customers to gain some control of their emotional state, allowing both customer and salesperson to move forward in the process of resolution. Second, echoing confirms your understanding; it makes sure that you are both talking about the same thing. By doing this, you reduce the risk of miscommunicating and making the situation worse. And third, echoing helps you and your customer to concentrate on the issue instead of on the emotions. You will find yourself less prone to feeling personally attacked.

When you've echoed the issue properly, the Customer from Hell has two basic responses available: 'Yes, that's right' and 'That's not what I said (or meant).' If the customer responds with 'Yes, that's right', then you've reassured him or her that you do, in fact, understand the problem. If the customer responds with 'No, that's not what I meant', then you've prevented a potential miscommunication.

Effective echoing requires some skill. If you don't do it properly, it can backfire on you. Following are three fundamental rules for echoing.

1. Echo the issue, not the emotion

As you are listening, customers will be communicating many things to you. They will be communicating their emotional state, their sense of frustration or anger, possibly their sense of betrayal or helplessness. They will also be telling you what the problem is and the situation surrounding it.

In the example I gave at the beginning of the chapter, the issue was that the blouse was a whole size smaller. One of the emotional comments from the customer, however, was 'Why don't you people get the information straight on the products you sell?' The customer had clearly put her faith in the salesperson and her knowledge of her products, and she was feeling betrayed.

As you listen, you will glimpse your customer's needs, situation, circumstances, personality and predispositions. It's entirely possible that your customer will talk, bellow, scream or rant for three or four minutes. Large chunks of what you hear will be manifestations of the emotional baggage the customer has brought in with him or her. It's not as easy as it may first appear to separate the real issue from all the rest of the information you are receiving. But if you don't, your echoing can lead to disaster.

Let's take another look at our example. What if the salesperson echoes 'There's no way you could wear it?' What is the message the customer might get? The customer might interpret this as 'So what if it shrank a bit? Of course you can still wear it.' Or she might hear 'Why don't you wear it anyway?' Either interpretation will lead only to an escalation of her emotional state. You see, when a customer says 'There is no way I can wear it now', she is expressing her sense of frustration. The problem is that the blouse shrank. The effect of that problem is that the customer can no longer wear the blouse.

What if the salesperson echoes 'You want to know why we don't learn more about our products?' The customer will probably hear that as a challenge. It will sound defensive or argumentative to her. The customer will then feel the need to defend her statement. Remember, when a customer says something like 'Why don't you people get the information straight on the products you sell?' she is expressing her sense of frustration that she put her trust in a salesperson who then let her down. She had positive expectations of the salesperson's ability, and now she feels betrayed.

Isolating the real issue to echo is a far greater challenge than it appears at first. You may not grasp the magnitude of the difficulty until you are actually in a conflict situation. A person may be screaming at you, bellowing, whining or crying. The person may be extremely confrontational, making you feel defensive. In such circumstances, it is very difficult to remain detached and logical. But the pleasant side effect of learning how to pierce through all of the miscellaneous information and concentrate on the key issue is that it does help you to keep your own emotional equilibrium. You are focusing more on what the actual problem is and less on the way this customer is affecting you.

Here are a couple of examples of things disgruntled customers might say. See how quickly you can determine the real issue.

Example 1: Everything's wrong

'Honestly, I don't even know why I use this firm of solicitors. This happens to me every single time! I'm telling you this document is two days late. Who does this stuff anyway, a school kid? I need it, and I need it now! I can't wait another day. And it can't have all the typos and mistakes you always have in your stuff. I have a buyer who is ready to sign right now, and he's going to get cold feet if I don't close the deal immediately. I'm paying you people a lot of money to do this work, and I expect high quality. You're the most expensive firm in the town, but I work with you because I thought you were the best. I suppose I was wrong!'

What is the issue here? Simply, it is that a document a customer needs to close a deal is taking too long to prepare. Several of the customer's statements – 'This happens to me every single time', 'Who does this stuff anyway?' and 'It can't have all the typos and mistakes you always have' – are simply expressions of the customer's frustration. It would be a huge mistake (and an easy one) to fall into the trap of addressing any one of them.

The proper way to echo the issue in this situation would be something like this: 'You have a buyer who is ready to sign right now?' Nice and simple, non-confrontational and no finger-pointing. You could say 'The document is two days late?', but then you might be setting yourself up for unwarranted blame. It's possible that the timing is perfectly reasonable but that the customer just thought the document could have been done faster. When echoing an issue, you must try to be as neutral as possible.

Example 2: The horrified host

'This meat is rancid! I have never been so embarrassed in my life. Here I was preparing for a dinner party, only to find that the main course was going to be ruined. I have half a mind to call the health department on you people. Have you no quality control? I can't believe you thought that you could get away with selling this. Do you think I'm stupid? My God, it's just fortunate that I've caught it in time, before I made all my guests sick.'

What's going on in the second example? Is the issue quality control? The customer's threat to call the health department? That the customer thought you were trying to 'get away with' something? Should you echo 'You've got half a mind?' No. The issue is that the meat the customer bought for an important dinner party was bad. And that's exactly how to echo it: 'The meat you bought here to serve at a dinner party was bad?'

The customer in each example has a right to feel frustrated. Regardless of who is to blame in each case, the customers have a right to feel frustrated. Echoing lets them know, without challenging them on the specifics of what happened, that you understand precisely why they are frustrated.

2. Watch your tone of voice

We've all heard the old saying 'It's not what you say but the way you say it', and I'll refer to it more than once in this book. And nowhere is this saying truer than in the case of echoing. Even when you're echoing the proper issue, the process will be counterproductive if the customer detects sarcasm, disbelief, surprise or anger in your voice.

Think again of the example of 'Everything's wrong'. The proper response for the employee in the firm of solicitors is 'You have a buyer who is ready to sign right now?' Just for fun, say that out loud. Say it with a really sarcastic tone of voice; then say it with disbelief in your voice. Now say it again with an angry tone of voice. Can you hear the difference? Can you understand the effect your tone of voice would have on someone?

Let's take this exercise one step further, just to make a point. Repeat this sentence out loud: 'That car is red.' On the whole, a pretty bland statement. Now use the same sentence to:

- express disgust over the colour;
- express surprise over the colour;
- express disgust about the car;
- express great happiness over the colour;
- express indifference about the colour; and
- make a point of the colour to someone for the third time.

Remarkable, isn't it? Tone of voice plays an enormous role in our society. When echoing, your tone is critical. For echoing to work, your customer must get the message clearly that you are listening and that you care.

3. Don't become defensive

Another common mistake we make in conflict situations is to become defensive or start providing explanations. Although providing an explanation may be valuable or necessary at some point, this is not the time to do it. Remember that what we want to do is let the customers have their say, make sure we understand exactly what it is they are saying and let them know we've heard it. Never try to 'explain' things to an agitated customer unless absolutely necessary. You will only be perceived as making excuses.

Perhaps the next worst thing you can do is to try to pass the blame back to the customer. If, in the example of the late document, the employee in the firm of solicitors replies 'Well, when did you get the information to us?' the customer will only become defensive, adding fuel to the confrontation.

When I'm conducting seminars on dealing with the Customer from Hell, I will occasionally, at this point, start getting 'Yes, buts'. 'Yes, but what if it is the customer's fault?' someone will ask me. 'Am I just supposed to let the customer get away with being rude?' Or 'Yes, but sometimes the customer is just being totally stupid!'

No, you don't have to let your customer get away with being rude, and, yes, sometimes customers are being totally stupid. You are well within your rights to stand up for yourself and 'straighten the customer out'. But here's a question: what is more important – ending a war or winning a war? There's no right answer; it's a personal choice. But if, deep down, winning conflict is more important to you than ending conflict, programmes such as this will never work for you. And you will always find yourself with more than your share of conflict.

At the echoing stage, you may well find yourself biting your tongue an awful lot, but if you are interested in ending the war it's worth it. It is difficult to put into words the effects that echoing can have on someone. You really have to try it and see for yourself. The changes in the other person's body language and attitude can be quite dramatic as the message – 'This person heard me, and understands' – sinks in.

Here again are the three keys to effective echoing:

1. Echo the issue, not the emotion.
2. Watch your tone of voice.
3. Don't become defensive.

8

Sympathizing with your customer

It is critical that your customer stop perceiving you as an opponent and start perceiving you as an ally.

In the listening and echoing processes, you have begun to break down some of the barriers between you and the customer. The customer is beginning to believe that maybe you do care, and the seeds of trust have been sown. You will find that by the time you've reached this stage (which, by the way, may take only a minute or two) the edge is off the customer's voice. The intensity has diminished considerably. You are still in conflict, but you are less and less in confrontation.

The next step is to reinforce and solidify the perception that you care. William Ury, in his book *Getting Past No*, refers to this process as 'stepping to their side'. It's a wonderful metaphor for the transition from confrontation to mutual problem-solving that takes place during conflict. But for this transition to take place, it is critical that your customer stop perceiving you as an opponent and start perceiving you as an ally. And the best way to accomplish this is by letting the customer know that you understand his or her situation and that you sympathize with what the customer is going through.

The operative word here is 'sympathize', not 'agree', and I can't make that point strongly enough. You don't have to agree with somebody's point of view to sympathize with how the person is feeling. Try saying something simple, such as 'From what you've told me, I can understand how you'd feel that way.' In saying this, you are conveying to the person that you understand his or her emotions. You aren't agreeing with the customer's position or opinions, but you are recognizing the emotional state and the customer's right to feel that way.

If you have truly listened to your customer, echoed the key issue back and put yourself in the customer's shoes, sympathizing with him or her isn't as difficult as you may believe. Remember my experience with Jane? Even the best of us, given a strong enough need, a desperate situation and a negative predisposition, can behave badly.

I should also stress that sympathizing does not mean apologizing. Apologizing, when required, is part of the final step of LESTER, the response. But there are times when apologizing is neither necessary nor appropriate. Be careful that you don't say 'I'm sorry that this happened to you' or 'I'm sorry that we messed up' or 'I'm sorry that you feel that way.' You don't want to apologize at this stage. What you do want to do is express understanding.

Take a look again at the words I used above: 'From what you've told me, I can understand how you'd feel that way.' What are the customer's options for a response to this statement? The customer may say 'Well, I hope so' or 'I'm sure you do' or 'So what are you going to do about it?' Or the customer may just break down and cry. (I've seen it happen more than once.) However the customer responds, I guarantee it will be far less confrontational than when you first saw him or her. If the customer does say 'So what are you going to do about it?' that's terrific. The customer is sending you the message that he or she has nothing further to say and is ready to begin resolving the problem.

One of my companies is RetailTrack, a mystery-shopping service. We have a network of investigators who discreetly visit our clients' shops and provide assessments of their customer service levels. Occasionally, a shop does not score well, and some shop managers can become quite defensive. Once, I was speaking to a group of about 200 shop managers, introducing the overall results of a recent mystery-shopping survey. One manager in the group was quite distressed over what she felt was a grossly unfair score, and she raised her hand to tell me so. I was faced with the same two options you are faced with in your business: do I address the problem right here and now, in a public forum, or try to find a more suitable venue for the discussion?

I told her that I took the issue seriously, that the integrity of the programme was paramount and that her concerns were very important to me indeed. I suggested to her that we speak together about it at the next break. She agreed.

To say that she was not very pleasant to listen to is an understatement. She was bitter and angry and extremely vocal. It turned out that she had received the lowest score in the chain and that the three employees on duty that day were all new and not yet up to speed. 'How am I supposed to motivate these people with you telling them that they are the bottom of the barrel?' she snorted.

As I patiently listened and prompted and echoed, I discovered that the employees had been hired to replace three people who had left, at short notice, to go to college. As a last resort, she had hired three of her daughter's best friends. They weren't working out at all, it seemed, but the manager couldn't discipline them or let them go without running the risk of alienating her daughter. This manager had made a fundamental mistake in her hiring practices, and she knew it.

Every bone in my body was screaming 'It's not our fault you hired the wrong people!' But with a great deal of effort, I decided to practise what I preach instead. 'From what you've told me, I certainly can understand your frustration', I said softly.

Her voice dropped so low I could barely hear it. She began to cry. 'I just don't know how to get out of this mess, and now, with this score, my supervisor thinks I'm a terrible manager.'

To cut a long story short, we were able not only to eliminate the conflict but also to resolve her employee problem that day, and I gained a lifelong friend.

So let's take a look now at how the first three stages of LESTER work. We'll start with a typical Customer from Hell experience:

Customer: I hate having to shop here! I wouldn't, you know, if it wasn't that my son is desperate for this toy and you're the only ones in this part of town who sell it!
Salesperson: [Uneasy silence.]

Customer: You people don't even care. You don't care about your customers. All you care about is making money from this junk you sell!
Salesperson: We care very much about our customers, madam.

Customer: You do not! You sell defective merchandise, which I'm constantly bringing back for refunds; your prices are much higher than every other place in town; and the people working here are rude!
Salesperson: I'm sorry, madam, but we really have no control over our suppliers' quality. We do, however, give refunds when there is a problem. And our prices are quite competitive.

Customer: Don't try to tell me about prices! Do you not think I shop around? I do, you know. And I don't need some part-time assistant to tell me that I don't know what I'm talking about!
Salesperson: [Giving up in frustration.] I don't set the prices, madam. I'm afraid you'll have to talk to my manager about that.

Customer: As though the manager's going to do something about it! All you people do is rip off people like me. It's all right, though – you'll learn your lesson when you go out of business.
Salesperson: Well, we've been around for 12 years. I hardly think –

Customer: I don't have time to argue with another rude assistant in this shop. Just forget it. And forget about this toy. I'll go across town and get it. [Customer stamps off.]
Salesperson: What's her problem?

Let's see how the same scenario might have played out had the salesperson followed the first three steps of LESTER:

Customer: I hate having to shop here! I wouldn't, you know, if it wasn't that my son is desperate for this toy and you're the only ones in this part of town who sell it.

Salesperson: *[Prompting.]* Really?

Customer: Yes, 'really'. I don't think I've ever bought a thing in this shop that I wasn't disappointed with – and the people here are really rude.

Salesperson: *[Prompting.]* Oh, no...

Customer: Yes. Sometimes I just want to scream. I don't mind paying the higher prices if I'm treated well, but I'm not. Half the time I'm just ignored.

Salesperson: *[Echoing.]* You've been ignored?

Customer: More times than I can count. And I just don't have the time to stand about waiting for someone to get around to me.

Salesperson: *[Sympathizing.]* From what you've told me, I certainly can understand how you'd feel frustrated.

Customer: 'Frustrated' isn't the word. In the past two months, my son has broken three toys, and I've had to bring them back. I was really made to feel like I was a nuisance.

Salesperson: *[Echoing.]* You've had toys break?

Customer: I know it's not your fault – you don't make them – but...

Do you see the change in the customer's attitude? The problem isn't solved yet, but the confrontation is gone. The real issue isn't price or defective merchandise; it's that the customer feels neglected and uncomfortable, and that's what's causing the conflict. But you had to listen actively to learn this.

Although I am presenting LESTER in a logical sequence, you'll notice that the listening and echoing activities continue throughout the process. Now you know why I spend so much time on these two elements. They are the essence of conflict resolution.

Sympathizing is an effective way to communicate to customers that you have truly listened and that you actually understand their situation. You don't have to agree – all you have to do is show respect for their position. In return, they will begin to believe that you may not be the enemy after all, and their confrontational attitude will begin to dissipate.

9

Thanking your customer

The package that complaints come in is unpleasant, yet what is inside is of critical importance to you and your business.

As odd as it may seem, that magical point where confrontation turns into active problem-solving is typically when you can say thank you to your customer.

'Let me get this straight', you're probably saying to yourself. 'I'm supposed to take this person who has been bellowing at me for the past five minutes and thank that person?' Well, yes. 'Do I really have a reason to thank this person?' you may ask. Again the answer is a resounding yes.

Here's a question for you. When most customers become dissatisfied with you, your products or your services, whom do they tell? You? No. They tell everyone but you. They tell their friends, acquaintances, business associates and sometimes even total strangers. At best, maybe 2 of every 100 dissatisfied customers actually take the time and have the inclination, the energy and the desire, or care enough about you and your business, to lodge a complaint with you or your company.

Think about it from your own perspective. When was the last time you wrote a letter to a manager? When was the last time you went into a shop to express your discontent over something? We just don't do it very often. The problem is, when nobody complains, people working in a business have no way of knowing they are doing less than a perfect job.

Yes, the package that complaints come in is unpleasant, yet what is inside is of critical importance to you and your business – it is information about your business and about how customers perceive you that 98 other people didn't bother telling you. And what did those other 98 people do? You know because you've done it yourself: they simply left and never came back. So a 'Thank you very much for taking the time to bring this to our attention' is legitimate, genuine and necessary.

These two Customers from Hell have also done something else that the other 98 people didn't bother doing: they've given you a second chance. They haven't 'defected' or walked away for ever and told all of their friends about their unpleasant experience. They've come to you and given you an opportunity to correct the situation. So you should also consider genuinely saying 'Thank you for giving us the opportunity to correct this situation.'

Think about how your customers are likely to respond after you've said something like that. In all probability, they'll look at you with a certain amount of astonishment and simply say 'You're welcome.' If they haven't said it already, they may even add 'Now what can we do about this?' Again, that's positive.

Whenever I take the time to fill out a company's comment or suggestion card, I'm always impressed when I receive a reply, particularly when the person makes a point of thanking me for taking the time to communicate with the company.

I spend about 200 nights a year in hotels. Over the years, I have stayed in some of the best and some of the scariest. Because of my experience, I tend to be very aware of the value and level of service I receive.

I once stayed at a posh, four-star hotel (which charged five-star prices). When I arrived, I was quite distressed to find myself in a check-in queue of five people, with only one person working at reception. This poor young receptionist had to deal not only with the queue but also with the telephones, and I had to wait almost 30 minutes before getting my room.

The receptionist was exceptionally pleasant and very apologetic for the delay. Nonetheless, paying over £150 per night with such slow service didn't sit well with me. Rather than give the receptionist a hard time – it wasn't his fault, after all – I chose to fill out one of the hotel's comment cards with some fairly pointed remarks.

To my surprise and delight, five days later I received a telephone call from the hotel's general manager, who handled the situation beautifully. He listened intently to my complaint, probing and prompting until I had it all out of my system. He then said 'Mr Belding, you had to wait 30 minutes?' I answered yes, to which he replied 'I certainly understand why that would upset you. It would upset me if I were in that position. It is quite distressing to me that your first impression of our hotel was one of inadequate service, and I want to thank you for bringing this to our attention. As you know, we are in a highly competitive business, and we can ill afford to have our customers perceive us in a poor light. If you hadn't informed us of your experience, we would never have realized there was a potential problem.' Did I feel good about that hotel after our conversation? I certainly did.

Thanking people is an acknowledgment of the value of their input. It reinforces that you care about them and that they are important to your business. It is at this point in conflict that more often than not something magical happens: the confrontation simply disappears. Rather than looking into the eyes of an enraged, frustrated customer, you are now looking into the eyes of somebody who perceives you as a friend, an ally.

Let's pick up our toy shop example from the previous chapter and see how this next element moves the whole process along:

Customer: I know it's not your fault – you don't make them – but it's really a nuisance bringing these things back. Particularly when I get told off by some young assistant.
Salesperson: [Echoing.] You've been told off for bringing something back?

Customer: Last week an assistant suggested that I should have called the manufacturer instead of bringing it into the shop. I don't want all that hassle. I thought you had a hassle-free return policy.
Salesperson: *[Thanking.]* We do, madam. Absolutely. Thank you very much for bringing this to our attention. The last thing we want is to make our customers uncomfortable.

Customer: Well, of course you don't. And most of the people in here are quite nice...

As you can see, the emotional states of the customer and the salesperson are now no longer part of the equation. The service person understands why the customer was frustrated, and the customer perceives the salesperson as an ally with whom she can talk. The stage is now set for a mutually beneficial solution to the problem.

Again, there are two valid reasons to thank your Customer from Hell. First, the customer is telling you things that most other customers won't bother to; second, the customer is giving you a chance to correct whatever is going wrong. Both are beneficial to you and your business.

10

Evaluating your options

Now is the time to think. Now is the time to sort out the options that are open to you.

It may not seem as if you've been very proactive so far. You've simply taken the brunt of your customer's emotional state. If you've followed the steps that I've outlined to this point, you've listened to the customer, encouraged the customer to talk more, echoed some of the key issues in the customer's mind, sympathized with the way the customer is feeling and thanked the customer genuinely for his or her input. You haven't actually resolved anything yet. What you have done, however, is successfully removed the negative emotional element from the equation.

At this point, the two of you are on the same team. You still have a problem to solve, but now you are able to do it together. This is the time to begin searching for what is commonly known as a win-win solution. Although it does require some effort on your part, a win-win solution is, more often than not, achievable.

The win-win approach

Although the phrase 'win-win' has been somewhat overused in the past few years, the concept is still sound. A win-win solution allows both people to leave a conflict believing that the solution was fair for each. Win-win is an attitude, a state of mind; it is not just a series of techniques one can use to solve problems. As I suggested earlier, to resolve conflict you have to want to resolve it. A positive resolution is one that leaves everyone satisfied.

Non-win-win attitudes or states of mind are thoughts such as 'How can I avoid losing?' and 'How can I teach this customer a lesson?' Even thoughts such as 'How can I appease this customer?' and 'How can I make this customer happy?' will not lead to a win-win solution. The thought process must be 'How can I resolve this to the benefit of both of us?'

Airlines, for example, use win-win solutions all the time. Let's say you go to check in for a flight. You've got a ticket, but the flight is overbooked. You're upset. Rather than simply turn you away, to have you defect to its competitor, the airline may move you into a first-class seat. The benefit to you is a comfortable trip to your destination. The benefits to the airline are no additional cost (the seat was empty anyway) and a satisfied customer who will keep coming back. If no first-class seat is available, an airline will often determine which customers are not in a great hurry and offer them a later flight in exchange for a complimentary ticket anywhere the airline flies. Those customers have the inconvenience of waiting, but they get the future benefit of a free flight. The airline, meanwhile, gains a happy customer, and all it had to give up was a seat on a flight that probably wouldn't have been full anyway. Everyone wins.

One Saturday afternoon in one of my toy shops, a customer showed up to pick up a large play structure for her son. Owing to a series of mistakes (mostly by me), the structure wasn't ready. When the customer found out it wasn't there, she was furious. Her son's birthday was the next morning, and she'd been promised it would be at the shop on Saturday for her to pick up. She had already paid for it, and she wanted her money back to go to another shop and get the product.

As I listened to her, I discovered that she lived 40 miles out of town and that she'd made a considerable detour on her way back from work to buy the product at our shop. She used our shop, she said, because she liked the service. The play structure was half an hour away in our warehouse, and she didn't have time to wait while I went to pick it up and bring it back to the shop. I listened, echoed her key issues, sympathized with her position and thanked her for bringing the problem to my attention. I then asked her what time the party would be. She told me that it would start at 11 am and was being held at a local café. I told her I'd gladly give her the money back if that's what she chose, but, if she preferred, I would drive out to her house myself and, while the children were at the café, erect the play structure in her garden so that it would be there as a surprise when they returned. She thought this solution was perfect.

The next day I delivered it and, just as an added touch, brought some gigantic red ribbon to wrap around it. That was a win-win situation. The customer got what she wanted. And I kept the sale and a long-term, valuable customer at a cost of three hours of my time and some petrol.

Think about the other options. What if I'd just given her the money back? That would have been a lose-lose situation. She would have been forced to go to another shop, consuming at least another hour of her valuable time with no guarantee that the second shop would have had the product either. I would have lost a sale, a valued, long-term customer and all of her friends.

What if my shop didn't have a cash return policy? What if I could offer only a credit note or an exchange? That could have led to a win-lose situation. I would have got to keep the money, but the customer would still not have had her play structure. The problem with a win-lose situation, of course, is that in the long run the 'winner' doesn't win at all. The customer would probably not have shopped in my shop again, and she still would have told all of her friends about her unpleasant experience.

I also could have overreacted, giving away a lot of free products. That would have been a lose-win situation. I would have been out an awful lot of money, and she would have walked away with an awful lot of products for her child. Perhaps keeping the customer satisfied by overreacting might have paid off in the long run. But there was a better solution, I believe, and that's the one I chose.

Probe for options

The evaluation stage is a time to probe for solutions acceptable to your customer. Tell the customer what some of your options are and see if any of them strike a chord. Get the customer involved in the creative resolution process.

Start off with some specific probing questions. You could say 'Mr Smith, you are a very valuable customer to us, and it is very important to us that you are satisfied. Would a refund be acceptable to you?' If this is an appropriate and viable option, Mr Smith will tell you so. If not, he will tell you that too, and he will usually tell you why it's not appropriate.

Let's take, for example, a customer who comes back into your shop to return a dress that has torn at the seams. You know by looking at it that the dress is too small for her. In fact, you remember selling it to her, and she was insistent on buying items two sizes too small. But now she is back in your shop complaining that you sell shoddy merchandise.

You listen intently to her complaint, echo the key issues and then say 'Well, Mrs Jones, from what you've told me, I can understand why you'd be frustrated. First of all, I'd like to thank you very much for bringing this to our attention and for giving us the opportunity to correct the situation. You're an important customer to us, and it's important to me that you are satisfied with everything in this shop. Would a refund be acceptable to you?'

To this Mrs Jones might reply 'I don't need a refund – I need a dress. I'm going out tomorrow night, and I don't have a dress to wear.'

You can then say 'Well, Mrs Jones, we do have some other beautiful dresses [larger, but you don't have to say that], and I'm confident you won't have this problem again.'

Then Mrs Jones might agree to look at the other dresses. Don't forget that it is your job, not the customer's, to search for options.

I purchased a new video cassette recorder on sale from a department store one Christmas. We struggled for three weeks to make it work and finally gave up when it ate a tape borrowed from a neighbour. I took the video cassette recorder back to the shop.

I explained to a very pleasant woman in the customer service department that an exchange would be great but that the first video cassette recorder still had my neighbour's tape in it. She pointed me towards the electronics department and told me that the salesperson there should be able to look after both the exchange and extracting the tape.

I arrived at the electronics department and explained again what had happened. The salesperson asked a few questions while filling out some sort of return form, then looked up at me and said matter-of-factly 'Well, we've got lots of machines, but you're not going to get your tape back.'

'What?' I asked, a little startled.

'Sir,' she said with a gentle scold and a you're-just-too-stupid-to-live expression, 'we don't repair these here. They get sent out for repairs. I've got eight machines already on their way. I doubt very seriously that the repair shop is going to send back a tape.'

Now, I hadn't walked into the shop prepared for a fight. I wasn't planning on being a Customer from Hell, but my back went up. 'I need that tape', I stated firmly. 'It belongs to a neighbour, and I have to return it.' I was not giving up.

The woman looked at me as if I'd sprouted another nose. 'Well, you're not likely to get it back from the repair place', she repeated. 'Once it's out of here, it's out of my control.'

'What if I open it up and take the tape out myself?' I asked.

Again the smirk and the head shake. 'You'll void the warranty.'

'Then give me the name of the repair place, and I will follow up to make sure I get back the tape', I persisted.

Again the shake of the head. 'If you want me to, I can give you the name of another place here in the city, and you can go and have your machine repaired yourself – still under warranty, of course. Then you'll probably get back the tape.'

'This video is brand new. I don't want it repaired. I want a new one!' I wasn't raising my voice yet, but I was really starting to lose my patience.

'Then you won't get back your tape', she said. She just stood there looking at me.

I matched her gaze and her silence.

After 30 seconds or so, she rolled her eyes and said 'I can call the manager if you like.'

I told her I thought that was a very good idea.

As we were waiting for the manager, the salesperson asked what tape it was.

'It's one of the *Star Wars* tapes,' I said. 'I'm not sure which one.'

'Well, we have the whole trilogy here', she said. 'If you had just told me that, I could have given you one of those in the first place!'

Three minutes later everything was settled. But not before I received one final scolding for not having a proper receipt.

Let's take a look at what happened here as it relates to LESTER so far. The salesperson listened to a certain degree as she was filling out the return form. She did not echo my key concerns, which caused me, later on in the discussion, to wonder if she in fact understood my predicament. She expressed no sympathy and certainly did not thank me. She made no effort to evaluate which options were open to her until I persisted. What she did, in fact, was go straight to the response stage. And the response, of course, was 'tough luck'.

If we assume she had done everything else right, what could she then have done in the evaluation stage? Which probing questions could she have asked? Here are three, just for starters:

▓ 'Is it a personal tape or a shop-bought one?'

- 'Would getting the machine repaired be acceptable to you, or do you definitely want a new one?'
- 'Would a replacement tape be suitable?'

You might argue that, since everything worked out in the end, what's the difference how I got there? I hope the answer is obvious. The difference is that I'm going to think twice before I go back there to shop. The difference is that the next time the customer may not be as well behaved as I was. The difference is that there is a better way. And look at the longer-term effects: I'm now writing about it in a book, and she probably went home that night to tell her husband about the Customer from Hell that day. Had she approached the situation with a win–win attitude, we both would probably have forgotten the transaction by the end of that day.

The most frequent mistake we make in managing difficult situations is that we tend to respond too quickly. We don't make a strong enough effort to thoroughly understand an issue and then explore all the options. Not only do we wind up contributing to the confrontation, but we also often find ourselves looking in the wrong places for solutions.

Think about the woman in the dress shop who had purchased an item too small for her. She was already embarrassed by having to return it, so why compound the problem by offering her an inappropriate solution?

Maintain control

Some people prefer the technique of just directly asking the customer to outline what it will take to fix the situation. 'What will it take to make things right?' Asking customers what they want or what they think will make the situation right has an interesting effect. First, customers will usually ask far less of you than you are prepared to give them. Second, with their emotional state now under control, they may actually be embarrassed to tell you what they really want.

But this is not the best approach, and you should use it only as a last resort. Look at it this way: if you leave it to customers to tell you what they want, you lose control of the situation and set yourself up for more potential conflict. If your customer becomes uncomfortable or embarrassed, then you have undone much of the good you accomplished in the first four stages.

It's not what you say...

The way you use language is critical in the evaluation stage. Returning to the example of Mrs Jones and the dress, notice that the salesperson said 'We do have some other beautiful dresses, and I'm confident you won't have this problem again.' A less skilled salesperson might have said 'We do have some other beautiful dresses, and I think if we get one a couple of sizes larger you won't encounter this problem again.' The thought is the same, but in the second example the message is 'You are fatter than you think you are.'

Being conscious of how you say things also means avoiding the temptation to scold your customer for having made a mistake or for not understanding your rules. This is particularly important when the customer's 'mistake' is actually the result of a salesperson not doing his or her job properly in the first place.

Earlier in this chapter, I suggested that a good way to start the probing process is to say something like 'You are a very valuable customer to us, and it is very important to us that you are satisfied...' It never hurts to be direct in telling customers how important they are (my daughter calls it 'sucking up').

I have a good friend and business partner who I believe would win Shameless Schmoozer of the Year Award. There is nothing he enjoys more than telling someone in no uncertain terms just how good he or she is. He lays it on with a trowel. And, the thing is, everyone loves Bob. In all the years I've known him, I've never heard anyone say 'I hate that guy when he says all those wonderful things about me!' Bob is honest, open and sincere with his praise. He also, not coincidentally, rarely finds himself in a confrontation.

The lesson from Bob, then, is don't be afraid to lay it on a little thick when telling customers how important they are. They won't object, I promise.

Don't make your customers feel stupid

Often, when a service person has not accurately determined a customer's needs, the customer will come back complaining that the product is defective or unsuitable. Many customers select an inappropriate product because it is less expensive, but they do not fully recognize that it will not suit their needs. They might buy too small a photocopier, or a two-door car when they really need a four-door car, or a one-week holiday instead of a two-week holiday.

Is this 'the stupid customer's own fault' for buying something that was wrong for him or her? No, it reflects a failure on the part of the original service person. And if the service person had outlined the risks of purchasing an inappropriate product in the first place, chances are the customer would not have come back angry, frustrated or unsatisfied.

I remember, for example, when I bought my first computer for business. In those days I had a choice between an XT, a 286 and a 386. The XTs were the slowest on the market and were quickly becoming outdated. The 386 had just been introduced and was considerably more expensive than the 286. The salesperson listened to what I would be using the computer for and recommended the 386. 'The 286 will do the job,' she said, 'but it probably won't be too long before most software will require the capabilities of a 386 simply to run. If you buy a 286, the chances are you will be coming back here within two years to upgrade. You may find it less expensive and more productive in the long run if you simply go with a 386 now.'

I decided this was simply part of the salesperson's spiel, took a chance and bought the 286. Sure enough, 18 months later, any new software I wanted to buy simply wouldn't run on my machine. I ended up having to buy a new one.

Oh, I was frustrated all right. And I was angry. But I was angry at myself for not having listened in the first place. When I went back to get my new computer, the salesperson resisted the temptation to make me feel even more stupid by saying something subtle, such as 'I told you so!' I appreciated that restraint. I picked out my new computer, and she recommended that I increase the memory capacity. This time I listened, and I was glad I did.

We must be certain, and should have very compelling reasons, before we start chastising our customers for making poor purchase decisions. For one thing, most purchase decisions should be influenced by a salesperson. And even when a customer knowingly makes a poor decision, it does no good to scold him or her for it. 'Well, madam,' the salesperson in the dress shop might have said, 'I told you not to buy a dress that small.' It doesn't do you any good to embarrass your customer.

Keep the end in sight

It is important during the evaluation process that you should not let your emotions get in the way. You might suspect, for instance, that a customer is lying to you or is just trying to pull the wool over your eyes. Even if you feel this way, you must think carefully about the impacts of your actions. Think about the value of that customer. If the customer walks away unsatisfied – even if he or she was lying to you – how many people is that person going to tell? Where are they going to shop after he or she tells them? How much business, in the long run, will this cost you?

Here again are the fundamental principles in evaluating the situation:

- Think win-win.
- Probe for details.
- Maintain control.
- Be careful how you say things.
- Don't make customers feel stupid.

11

Responding to the situation

The secret is not to let the guidelines, rules or lines of authority stand in the way of resolving the situation. Sometimes this means you have to be creative.

Once you have evaluated the situation and determined the options open to you and the options suitable to your customer, you must respond. Now is the time to solve the problem. Now is the time to act.

As I've noted, the most common mistake service people in difficult situations make is to jump straight to this stage, ignoring the five previous steps. Interestingly, there is one other type of service person who rarely, if ever, reaches this stage. This is the Order Taker, who takes down all the information, promises to pass the complaint along, but never actually does anything about it. Then there are the Dismissers, those who evaluate the situation and determine what the response should be, but don't bother following through because it's just going to be too much hassle.

A wonderful illustration of the importance of responding effectively, instead of being non-responsive, occurred when I was having a problem with my laptop computer. The whole story unfolded over a six-week period. I was in a large city, hundreds of miles from my home, meeting some of our existing clients and preparing for a huge presentation to a prospective new client. My two-year-old laptop chose that moment to die on me, with this vital presentation locked inside it.

Needless to say, I was more than a trifle worried. I dug up the phone number of the manufacturer's 24-hour service line, negotiated my way through the intricate voicemail system and finally managed to get a living, breathing human being on the line. The young man (at least he sounded young) was fabulous. He started off by doing a nifty little over-the-phone diagnosis of the computer and determined that the problem was a 'CMOS register test failure'. He then explained to me that this was usually an indication that the computer's motherboard – the heart of the computer – had failed. 'There is a slim chance,' he added, 'that it's just that the CMOS battery is dead, in which case it's not a serious problem at all.' He continued to advise me on the procedure for having the computer repaired, which began with 'First you package the computer in a box and send it to…'.

When I explained my situation to him and informed him that I needed a solution within the next 30 hours, there was a pause at the other end of the line. With a tremendous amount of empathy in his voice, he said 'Mr Belding, our company doesn't have a procedure or a system in place for solving problems that quickly, and there's really not much I can do at the moment. I do understand your situation, though. What I can do, perhaps, is give you some other options for having it fixed.' He then listed four or five things I could try, but made it clear that he wasn't sure any of them would work. 'Good luck!' he said at the end.

When I hung up, I was feeling pretty good. The representative had listened carefully, quickly identified that my biggest problem at the moment was time, and let me know that he sympathized with my situation. He had then demonstrated that he cared by providing a number of possible solutions that fell well outside company policy. Wow! I thought. This company really gets it! Unfortunately, that thought lasted for only a few minutes.

I began to follow up on the representative's suggestions. One of the next calls I made ended up being re-routed all the way back to the same call centre the first representative worked in. I won't go into the details of what ensued, but suffice it to say that I had perhaps the worst customer service experience of my life. I was scolded for attempting to find alternative channels for having my computer fixed. I was told that the first representative was incompetent and should never have given me the options he did. I was told that there was no possible way to have my computer fixed in a 30-hour period and that, if I tried to have someone outside the company fix it, I might be in Serious Trouble.

Over and over again, I explained that this presentation was important to me, that money was no object and that I was simply looking for whatever suggestions anyone could offer. Over and over again, the second representative made it clear that I was a huge pain in the backside. Finally, in exasperation, I said 'I don't think you understand. I'm 500 miles from home, I have a critical presentation to give in a day and a half, and I've got a damn computer that won't work!' He hung up on me.

He was a Dismisser, someone who had no interest in making my problem his. The worst part of the story, however, is still to come. I decided to get hold of a supervisor to let someone know how I had been treated. After leaving six messages for various supervisors and managers, all of which went unanswered, I wrote a letter to the managing director. At this point, I was no longer upset (I'd had the computer fixed by a local dealer for £30), but I thought that the MD might appreciate knowing about this chink in the company's armour.

Six weeks later, I got a call from a local manager to whom my letter had finally drifted. He listened to my story, and I told him of the unanswered telephone calls. He thanked me very much for my input, told me that customer service was very important to the company and said that he would make a report about this incident for his boss. That was it. He took the order.

Although he had followed most of the steps of LESTER and was very pleasant, I still felt a little... well... unsatisfied. Something was missing. He didn't give me a sense of closure, of completeness. After all the time that had gone by, it wasn't enough.

Respond instantly

The first rule of responding is to respond instantly. Statistics show that more than 75 per cent of complaining customers will remain customers if you solve the problem. But more than 90 per cent will remain customers if you solve the problem instantly.

This rule often poses a problem because many companies do not give their employees a great deal of discretion. It may be that what the customer wants can be approved only by the supervisor, manager or head office. In some companies, even the managers do not have many options for satisfying their customers. Still, the last thing you want to do is push the problem away. Even if you are in this situation, you can still respond instantly. You might not be able to solve the problem instantly, but you can respond to it instantly. What you need to communicate to your customer is that you don't have the authority to resolve the situation but that you are going to take it upon yourself to make sure that it gets resolved.

If you aren't the ultimate decision maker, try saying something like this: 'This is something my manager usually looks after, but it is very important to me that you are satisfied. If it is OK with you, I would like to get your name, telephone number and address so that I can personally see to it that this gets resolved.' This approach reinforces for the customer that you do truly care and that you are on the customer's side. It also saves the customer from having to justify his or her position to yet another person.

In difficult situations, customers are looking for signs that you care. Most rational people will understand when something is beyond your control or authority. Most people understand that you have to operate within guidelines established by your company, just as they do with the companies they work for. The secret is not to let the guidelines, rules or lines of authority stand in the way of resolving the situation. Sometimes this means you have to be creative.

A wonderful story was related to me by the manager of a large shopping centre who had purchased a carpet shampooer from a major, well-known department store. He wrestled the large box that the shampooer came in to the till, paid for it and took it home. One week later, the same shampooer in the same store went on sale for 20 per cent less. He went to the store with his receipt to see if it would credit him the difference. The woman at the customer service desk informed him in no uncertain terms that sale prices applied only to merchandise purchased during the sale period. Although she didn't say it in exactly these words, the message was 'Tough luck'.

My friend then asked if he could return the product and get his money back.

Absolutely, she said. The store had a no-hassle, money-back guarantee.

My friend, becoming somewhat agitated, then said, 'OK, so you are telling me that I have to bring the product back, get my money refunded and then go and pick out a new one and purchase it at the sale price?'

She looked at him as if he was a con artist but said, 'Well, I suppose you could do that.'

So he drove back to the house, picked up the shampooer, drove it back to the store, went to the 'customer service' desk (interesting name for it, given the circumstances) and got a cash refund for the product. He then carried the product back to the checkout and repurchased it at the sale price.

Technically, the woman at the customer service desk did nothing wrong. She was following the rules and regulations set by her company – rules and regulations over which she had no control. The creative solution to the problem, however, would have been for her simply to give him the cash difference and then ring through both the return and the new sale on her terminal after he was gone. The net outcome would have been the same for the store but much more positive for the consumer. The best solutions, win-win solutions, are almost always creative solutions.

Think of union negotiations. One side takes posture A; the other side takes posture B. The ultimate solution is almost never A or B, nor is it a compromise – something between A and B. The win-win solution is usually something entirely different: C, D, E or F.

When appropriate, own up

If, after you've listened to your customer, it turns out that you have actually done something wrong, don't be afraid to swallow your pride and accept responsibility. Tell your customer you made a mistake. Let the customer know it was entirely your fault (if it was). Don't make excuses or give the customer 'good reasons' about why it happened. Simply accept responsibility.

If it was someone else who made a mistake, then accept responsibility on behalf of the company, but don't point your finger at the other service person. In other words, don't say 'Yes, you are right. Sheila really messed up this time.' Now is the time for the royal 'we'. 'Yes, you are right. We really messed up this time.' If the customer perceives you to be passing off blame to someone else, you will lose credibility instantly.

Following up

The final principle of responding is perhaps the most important because this is your opportunity to turn what is a negative situation into a positive one. It is your chance to turn a potentially 'defecting' customer into a long-term, loyal patron of your company. This final principle is to follow up, which is especially important if you have to pass off a decision to the manager.

Consider this situation. A customer is irate because the widget he'd ordered from your company hasn't been delivered yet. There is nothing that you, the employee, can do about it, but you say that you will certainly bring it to the attention of your manager. You do, and the manager responds by sending the widget to the customer that day and then informing him of the action that has been taken.

What if, one week later, you phone the customer and say 'Hello, Mr Jones, it's Shaun Belding calling from Acme Widgets. I was the one you spoke to about the widget delivery. I was just calling to see if everything was resolved to your satisfaction.'

How do you think your customer will respond to this? He'll probably think 'They really do care!' Do you suppose he'll tell his friends about his experience? Of course he will, but now it will be in a positive light instead of a negative one.

By following up on a difficult situation once it has been resolved, you solidify your relationship with your customer and, at the same time, make yourself an ambassador for your company. Such ambassadors cannot be replaced by all the advertising in the world.

There are thus three keys to responding:

▪ Respond instantly.
▪ Be honest.
▪ Follow up.

And that's LESTER. It's a simple, effective process that can help you through most difficult situations. It doesn't work all the time, but, like anything else, the more you practise it, the better you become at it.

▪ **Listen:** Learn about both the situation and the customer. Let your customer know that you care.
▪ **Echo:** Reflect back the key points to let the customer know you understand the situation.
▪ **Sympathize:** Step to your customer's side. Although you may not agree with the customer, let the customer know that you respect his or her point of view.
▪ **Thank:** Let your customer know that you appreciate his or her feedback.

▨ **Evaluate:** Try to find a solution acceptable to everyone involved.

▨ **Respond:** Deal with the situation as fast as you can, and make sure it is to your customer's satisfaction.

12

The unreasonable customer

The number of customers who are truly unreasonable is very small indeed.

Let's try to put this into perspective. In the world of Customers from Hell, many of the situations are taken care of effectively by using the principles of LESTER. Many will also simply disappear as we become better service people – as defined in Chapter 3 of this book. This leaves us with a handful whom we can call unreasonable customers.

If we agree that Customers from Hell are a tiny minority of the total number of customers we see each year, then the number of customers who are truly unreasonable is very small indeed. We do encounter them from time to time, however, and this chapter is dedicated to techniques for dealing with them.

The unreasonable customers are listed in no particular order. Unlike LESTER, which applies globally to unsatisfied customers, the solution to each type of unreasonable customer behaviour is unique. So far as I have been able to determine, there is no single sure-fire method for handling all the different types of unreasonable customers.

The time vampire

Sandy, a new employee in one of my toy shops, had just come in for her usual 6 pm shift and was telling me about her experience of the night before. It seemed that a customer had kept her a full hour past closing time.

'Are you mad?' I said to her. 'Why didn't you just tell her to leave?'

'I tried,' said Sandy, 'but I just couldn't get her to go.'

I harrumphed a bit at that, muttered something about being more assertive, and wandered off shaking my head.

Two days later, I met the same customer, and the same thing happened to me. I remember dropping subtle hints – 'I think I'd better lock up the shop' – and then trying direct hints such as turning off most of the lights in the shop and counting the cash. All this woman did was talk and talk and talk. In the hour and a half that she was there, I learnt all about her children, her husband, many of the medical ailments she had, and every good deed she had done since she was six years old. It didn't seem to matter what I said or did; nothing dissuaded her.

That woman was a time vampire. We meet them in all shapes and sizes. Sometimes they are friends who come in to visit us when we're trying to work. Sometimes they are customers who want to socialize with us when we're busy. Time vampires are both a tremendous source of frustration and a real liability to a business.

After my little episode, I took it upon myself to learn how to deal with this type of Customer from Hell. It took a lot of painful trial and error, but I finally came up with a solution that works most of the time. The first thing is to understand what makes these people time vampires. What motivates them? Well, chances are they're lonely and have a desperate need to be heard. They have a tremendous lack of social skills and no understanding of some of the basic social graces. But the most important thing to be aware of is that they do not recognize that their actions are inappropriate. They confuse politeness on the part of the service person with a desire to listen to them. They perceive hints such as 'It's almost closing time' as a desire on your part to share information. Like most social faux pas, the behaviour is neither deliberate nor malicious.

Time vampires are almost always self-focused. They are completely unaware of your needs and your perception of the situation. They also have you at a disadvantage because they're playing by social rules (their own) that are completely different from the ones with which you are familiar.

The solution to handling a time vampire is easy intellectually. It does require, however, breaking some of the social rules you grew up with, and doing so can be quite an emotional challenge. The solution may also at first appear harsh to you. It will probably go against your most basic sense of what is right and what is wrong, what is socially acceptable and what is not. The key, though, is to remember that these people are not getting the subtle clues. Subtlety doesn't work with time vampires.

What does work is being brutally direct, even abrupt – almost to the point of being rude. Believe it or not, a 'gentle clue' to a time vampire is the equivalent of a club on the head for most people. It's a three-step process:

- **Gentle Clue 1** is to put a physical barrier between the two of you. You accomplish this with body language. Interrupt the person. Put both of your hands in front of you, as if to push the person away. Look into his or her eyes. Let the person know in no uncertain terms that it is your turn to talk. If your time vampire is on the telephone, interrupt her with 'Excuse me'. You may have to say it a few times before she stops talking.
- **Gentle Clue 2** is then to say something direct and frank, such as 'I'd love to keep talking to you, but I am afraid that you will have to leave.' On the phone, you might say 'I'd love to keep talking to you, but I have to go.'
- **Gentle Clue 3** is instantly to turn your back on the time vampire (before he or she has a chance to say anything) and walk away. If it's closing time, walk to the door and wait for the person to come out with you. If the person

is in your office, walk through the door and wait for him or her to follow. If you are on the phone, finish with 'If there is anything else I can do, please call.' Then hang up.

Simple, isn't it? Right. If somebody treated you this way, you would surely find this as offensive as I would. But trust me on this one: time vampires will not find it offensive in the least. In fact, the beauty of this technique is that, each time they come back (and they will come back), the clues you have to leave them become subtler and subtler. While they may never actually understand why you can't spend all that time with them, they will begin to recognize the pattern.

I don't want to leave you with the impression that time vampires are all stupid. They're not. Many time vampires I've met are highly intellectual people who are either insecure or just socially unskilled. I expect they would be devastated if they knew how much of a challenge they are to people and how much of a negative impact they have on a business.

The permissive parent

If you're a retailer, chances are you've met a parent who seemingly has no control over his or her child. The child runs rampant through the shop, destroying displays, pulling merchandise off shelves and being a general annoyance to your other customers. I list such a parent as an unreasonable customer because he or she unreasonably expects that you and your other customers should accept that kind of behaviour from the child.

It's a tough situation to deal with. On the one hand, you don't want someone's child disrupting the shop or damaging merchandise. But on the other hand, you don't want to offend a parent who is, presumably, a customer. Nevertheless, you have to do something. The cost of not acting can be too great. It is not just that there is a great potential for the child to do serious damage, either to him- or herself or to the shop, but also that there is a real negative impact an untamed child can have on other customers.

If the other customers in the shop become irritated, they will not have a pleasant shopping experience. If they do not have a pleasant shopping experience, they are far less likely to make a purchase and will remember that unpleasant experience the next time they consider going to your shop. If you don't at least attempt to resolve the situation, you run the risk of having your customers leave your shop thinking 'Why didn't they do something about that child?' or 'How could they let that child run wild like that?' In the minds of the customers, 'they' includes you.

I think we all recognize that the child is most often not really the problem. Young children generally act within the parameters set by their parents. In the child's mind, what he or she is doing is acceptable because the parents have never said that it isn't. It's also likely that the parents take no action because they believe that everyone else finds their child and his or her actions as 'cute' as they do.

It is also possible, of course, that it's not the child at all. The problem just might be your own low tolerance level for children. In all fairness, some people are distressed by everything children do. If you have a low tolerance level for children and the way they behave generally, don't assume that other people feel the same way. Before you take action, be sure that the child is actually disturbing other people or doing something that is destructive to the shop. It is important that you make the distinction between a boisterous, happy child and one who is causing mischief. If, however, the child is creating a disturbance that is affecting the other customers, they will certainly appreciate your taking action. Their frustration will increase if you do not take action.

There are two effective ways of dealing with an uncontrolled child. They seem to work equally well depending on your personality. The first one is to make a joke out of it. I had a young man working for me who was adept at this light-hearted technique. He would bound up to a child who was busily tearing merchandise off the shelf, squat down in front of the child and, with a big smile and a voice loud enough for the parent and the other customers to hear, say 'Why are you tearing my shop apart?' The child would usually answer with only a big grin, but inevitably the parents would recognize that the child had been doing something inappropriate and pull in the reins.

Obviously, this light-hearted approach is not one that everyone would be comfortable using. Nor is it a technique that everyone could execute credibly. The successful use of this approach requires a very outgoing, confident personality. If you're comfortable with being light-hearted, then try it. If you're not comfortable with this approach, then don't.

The second method, for those who prefer a more conservative approach, is to confront the parent directly and express concern for the safety of the child. You can say 'Oh, excuse me, but I'm just a little concerned about your child. He may pull one of those racks over on top of himself, and I'd hate to see him get hurt.' Whether parents see through this façade is unimportant. What is important is that it works and that it allows parents to save face in front of the other customers and you.

The sexual harasser

Sexual harassment from a customer, which fortunately is very rare, is an extreme type of negative behaviour. One could easily fill the pages of this book with nothing but strategies to manage sexual harassment. And in fact many excellent books have been written on the subject. If you are experiencing any form of sexual harassment, I recommend you seek out appropriate resource people for advice. It is not something to take lightly.

If I can pass along one important rule of thumb, however, it is this: if you are being sexually harassed by a customer, remove yourself from the situation instantly. Don't apologize; don't explain; don't excuse yourself. Simply walk away and go directly to somebody in authority, such as a manager. If you are alone in the reception area, simply leave to find someone in authority. Don't worry about phone calls not getting answered. If you are alone in your shop, then leave the shop and seek out somebody in security. Don't worry about people stealing things because you've left. There is no phone call or stock in the world worth more than your emotional and physical well-being. I would even go so far as to say that, if your manager or supervisor does not agree with this philosophy, seek employment elsewhere with someone who cares about you. If you are a manager, your role in supporting your employees is critical. If someone comes to you complaining about being sexually harassed by a customer, do not take it lightly. Act immediately.

Having said all this, I recognize that dealing with sexual harassment is easy to put on paper but not so easy to put into practice. Walking away from a customer goes against everything we've ever been taught. Not only will you think that you're being rude, but you will also be losing a customer and all of the customer's friends. It's not easy to do. All I can tell you is that walking away beats the alternatives.

As a retail manager, I had to deal with the sexual harassment of one of my staff, and the experience left a lasting impression on me. There was a man who frequented one of our shops and whom we knew only as 'Paul's father'. He was an abrasive man with a booming voice and an untamed four-year-old child. We always had advance notice that Paul's father was coming into our shop because Paul (not his real name) usually preceded him by about five minutes.

Every time the routine was the same. Paul would run into the shop and head straight for the play area. Five minutes later his father would walk into the shop, stand 4 feet inside the front door, and bellow 'Paul? Paul? Where are you, Paul?' All the while he would look around, making sure that people were noticing him. He rarely, if ever, purchased anything, but he consumed much of our staff's time by asking a lot of Very-Important-Sounding Questions. I thought of him simply as a nuisance and a boor and thus paid little attention to him.

One evening, at a restaurant where I was hosting an informal employee recognition dinner, the subject of Paul's father came up in casual conversation. Apparently, he'd been making some rather bold remarks to one of my young employees. She considered him a harmless, if obnoxious, idiot and spent 15 minutes telling us stories. She thought it was a big joke and had us all in hysterics as she told us about some of the stupid things he did. 'He was in this afternoon', she said with a chuckle. 'He just walked straight up to me, stared at my breasts, said "Ooh-la-la", and then walked away. This guy's got to get a life!' When I asked her if he was bothering her, she just laughed and said 'No, I've seen a lot worse.' So I put Paul's father out of my mind.

About a month later, the young woman who'd been the object of Paul's father's affection left to go to college full time, at which time Paul's father shifted his attention to another young employee. She didn't find him nearly as amusing. 'What an idiot!' she said to me at one point in exasperation. 'Can I tell him to get lost?'

Right then I made a classic managerial mistake. Because the first employee had dismissed Paul's father as a harmless moron and considered his behaviour a joke, so did I. As a result, I didn't take the second employee's complaint seriously. That is, until a week later, when she phoned me at home in tears asking me again for permission to tell him off. It was then that I realized how profoundly Paul's father was affecting her and how helpless she must have felt when I failed to respond the first couple of times she'd brought the problem up. I promised her that I'd deal with the situation the next time he came into the shop.

I was now faced with a dilemma. First, he'd never made any of these comments in my presence. Second, his comments had been restricted to innuendo and subtle suggestion. In confronting him, I had no specific statements I could use to support my position. If I was challenged on the specifics, I could only reply that he'd told one of my employees that her sweat-shirt really looked nice on her. Third, given Paul's father's loud and obnoxious manner, I knew it could easily escalate into an unpleasant scene. Nevertheless, I refused to allow anybody to abuse one of my employees.

So I planned my strategy, and when he came through the door two days later I took a deep breath and confronted him. I asked if I could speak to him for a moment, and then ushered him discreetly out the front door of the shop to a quiet corner outside. I was direct and blunt with him. 'I've had some complaints from my employees about some of the things you are saying to them', I began. 'And these comments are making my employees extremely uncomfortable. I'm afraid I have to ask you not to come into my shop any more.'

I steeled myself for a loud and accusatory 'What the hell are you talking about?' but it never came. Instead, he took a small step back. His eyes started darting to and fro. He backed away, talking under his breath like a scolded child. 'Oh, I didn't know', he mumbled. 'I had no idea.' And with that he turned and walked away. We never saw him again.

I have since had several other similar encounters. And, as a manager, I have learnt one valuable lesson about sexual harassment: when confronted by an authority figure, the sexual harasser will usually back down. When not confronted by an authority figure, the sexual harasser will continue his or her behaviour. This means that, if you are being harassed, you need to get someone in authority involved. And, if you are a manager, you must respond to your employees' needs immediately.

The bully

As is the case with sexual harassers, people who physically threaten service people are an extreme type of Customer from Hell. Fortunately, these customers are also rare. They should, however, be handled carefully. People who physically threaten or use physically threatening body language are emotionally troubled and can be quite unpredictable.

If you ever find yourself feeling physically threatened, there is but one objective, and that is to protect yourself. The best strategy, as with sexual harassment, is to remove yourself instantly from the situation. Again, don't apologize, don't excuse yourself, don't explain yourself – just quickly remove yourself from the customer's presence and find someone in authority. If you are by yourself, find somebody in security, or dial 999 and ask for the police. This is not the time to be concerned about looking foolish or overreactive. I've heard many stories of physically abusive customers that have sent chills up and down my spine.

An accounts assistant for a manufacturing company once told me of a customer who came to her office and then followed her home. A cashier I met in a training session told me of a situation that had happened the day before, when a customer had literally tried to jump across the counter because he thought she'd rung something up incorrectly. A salesperson in an upmarket women's clothing shop once described to me how she'd been pinned against a wall by an irate husband who'd wanted a cash refund.

With the bully, the best strategy is to remove yourself from the situation rather than try to fix it. Don't, for example, take this as an opportunity to scold the customer about his or her behaviour. If you have a physically abusive customer in an agitated state and you turn and say 'I find your behaviour quite inappropriate', you are only asking for trouble. As a rule, these people aren't used to dealing with situations intellectually. Just get away.

Foul mouth

At one time or another, most of us have encountered a customer who has chosen to use foul language when dealing with us. Although I am presenting this person as an unreasonable customer, LESTER will usually help you to deal with the situation. I bring up the swearing customer separately because sometimes we respond to these people in a fashion that can be very counter-productive and only intensify confrontation.

Customers swear in difficult situations for really only one reason: they are frustrated, and swearing is the only way they know how to express themselves. For many, it is simply a normal way of speaking. Let's face it, we've all met people who can't seem to put a single sentence together without using a four-letter word. Confronting them by saying 'Please don't swear' will only make matters worse. If swearing happens to be part of a person's normal way of speaking, then that person will perceive it as a personal criticism. If the person is swearing because he or she is fed up to the teeth, scolding the person isn't going to make life any easier for either of you.

When somebody swears during a difficult situation, just ignore it. Listen intently to what the problem is, echo the key issues (without the swear words, of course), sympathize with the customer and thank the customer for his or her input. You'll find that, if you have adequately controlled your own emotional state and followed the first four steps of LESTER, the customer will often correct his or her own behaviour. Remember that, once you have removed the confrontational aspect of conflict and stepped to the customer's side, the customer's emotional state will begin to settle down. Often, if you've handled the situation properly, the customer will turn to you and say 'I'm sorry for the way I was talking. I'm just so frustrated.'

Most swearing customers know that what they are doing is wrong, and they know that it is inappropriate. But they don't know how to react any better. In those rare situations when the swearing is intense or is directed at you personally, it becomes more difficult to ignore. When this happens, you should, rather than scolding the customer, try to put the customer's behaviour into the context of the issue at hand. Let the customer understand in a gentle way that you want to address the problem but that his or her behaviour is making it difficult for you to function.

So instead of saying 'Please don't swear', try saying 'I really want to resolve this as best I can, but when you speak to me like that I just can't think straight.' This response places the emphasis on your interest in resolving the issue rather than on the customer's behaviour. It doesn't work in all cases, but it minimizes the risk of magnifying the conflict.

Hell's accountant

Some customers just love to tell you how much more expensive your products are than those of your competitors. At one of our toy shops, we had one customer who used to come in once a week. She was a good customer and spent hundreds of pounds with us. But every time she came into the shop, she made a point of telling us how much cheaper some of our products were at our competition. She drove us mad. I used to make excuses and explain our prices by saying 'Well, yes, they probably do have products that are less expensive than ours, just as we have products that are often less expensive than theirs.'

It took me a while, but I finally realized that she wasn't doing this to upset me or belittle the shop; rather, as a loyal customer, she thought that it was her responsibility to advise me about what the competition was doing. I eventually learnt to say, simply, 'Oh, really? Thank you very much for letting me know.' She would smile and say 'Well, I know it's important to you to know what other people are doing.'

Of course, not all customers tell you about a competitor's lower prices out of a sense of loyalty. They often follow their statements by asking if you will match the other shop's prices. If your shop does not price-match and this happens, there are a couple of different strategies you can use. The easiest is to smile nicely and say 'Oh, I would love to, but I don't have the authority to do that. I can get the manager, however. You are welcome to speak to her.'

What this approach does, first of all, is let customers know that you are on their side and that you are willing to do your part to satisfy them by getting the person who has the authority to make pricing decisions. About half of the customers will respond 'Oh, no, never mind' and make the purchase anyway. They do this because they're as uncomfortable with confrontation and negotiation as you are. The downside to this strategy is that you are saying, in effect, 'I don't want to deal with you' and passing the customer off to someone else. As I've discussed, this response can make people uncomfortable.

A better strategy is to deal with the situation proactively. You don't want to apologize for your prices (they pay your wages, after all), but you also don't want to make your customers feel cheap for having tried to negotiate with you. Simply thank them for their input, let them know you are on their side, and reassure them that your prices are fair. Try saying something like this: 'My, that is an excellent price, and I appreciate your letting us know. I'd love to help, but our shop has a long-standing policy of not matching prices because we believe it wouldn't be fair to the customers who have paid full price. Our prices are competitive, however, and we'll be around should you ever have a problem.'

This approach thanks customers for their input, reiterates the policy while gently explaining the rationale for it and then reassures the customers that they are getting good value. If you have the courage, it is always best to end your statement by trying to close the sale. You could say, for example, 'Which colour would you prefer?' or 'Would you like to get any of the accessories with that?' You'll be amazed at how many customers will simply drop the issue and make the purchase.

Customers often raise the issue of price, but research shows that price is a primary motivation in less than one out of four purchase decisions. If your customer service has been superior to that of the other company, three out of four people will pay the higher price and purchase the item from you. When they ask you about price, they are usually just saying 'Reassure me that I'm getting good value.'

Mistaken Mary

At some point, a customer is going to call you or walk into your shop or office with a product you've never seen before and ask to return it or have it fixed. The conflict usually starts when the service person looks at the product and says 'No, you didn't buy this here', making the customer feel a little stupid.

Some people aren't comfortable with the possibility of being wrong, and they will react by asserting that it must be you, the service person, who's mistaken. The key to preventing confrontation is in the first words you say. So rather than saying 'No, we don't sell that', start by saying 'Oh, goodness, I haven't seen this before. Do you remember how long ago it was that you purchased it?' Or 'Do you by any chance have your receipt?' After the customer has answered (this customer never has a receipt, of course), double-check that your company hasn't sold that product before. The next step is to return to the customer with a problem-solving answer instead of just a flat no.

For example, you might try saying 'I wonder if you could have purchased this from XYZ company. We often get confused with them.' Don't risk embarrassing customers. Give them an opportunity to bow out gracefully. If they remain adamant, however, make sure that they understand you are not arguing with them. Make a point of checking with your colleagues and the files. Say to the customer 'Well, you may very well be right. Let me just double-check again.' Do everything in your power to let customers know you are on their side.

Sometimes customers will try to return something that your company does carry but that they purchased from a competitor. They could be doing it because your company charges more for it and they think they can make a few pounds on it by returning it this way. More likely, though, it's just more convenient for them to return it to you.

Unless your company has a strict policy of not accepting returns without receipts, I recommend you take the product back with a big smile and don't make an issue of it. Yes, you might lose a few pounds in the transaction, but you stand to make it back a hundredfold over the years with satisfied customers.

Wishy-washy Wendy

There are some people in this world who simply can't make up their minds. They'll dilly-dally and drone on, saying 'Well, I'm just not sure.' When you hear this, one of two things has happened – either they need reassurance or you haven't closed the sale.

1. They need reassurance

Indecisive customers are often looking for reassurance about their purchases. The tricky part is trying to determine precisely what they need reassurance about. Sometimes they are so vague that trying to divine the roadblock is like trying to put tooth-paste back into the tube.

Start by restating your understanding of the customer's needs and outlining why you believe your recommendation is appropriate. Say, for example, 'You indicated that you are hoping to find a CD player for your daughter. You wanted something portable and durable, but you didn't want to spend a lot of money. From what you've told me, I think this particular model would suit your needs perfectly.'

The next step is a direct question, such as 'Is there something I've missed? What is it you're unsure about?' Now comes the tricky part. Indecisive customers aren't comfortable telling you what they are unsure about. Once you have asked the questions, you must be very patient, listen very, very carefully and read between the lines. You might have to ask some specific, probing questions: 'Are you comfortable with the brand? Are you comfortable that this will do the job for you? Is it within your budget?'

At some point, indecisive customers will probably say 'Oh, it's just a little thing really...' or 'Oh, I know it's no big deal, but...', and that's your clue. When indecisive customers tell you it's no big deal, you know it is huge in their minds.

You see, indecisive customers are often so concerned with making a mistake that it paralyses them. They continually run 'what if?' scenarios through their minds. What if I get home and find I paid too much for it? What if I get home and my husband gives me grief for it? What if it becomes obsolete in three months? What if, what if, what if?

The first thing to be aware of is that, if you in any way trivialize their concerns, you will lose them instantly. Let them know that you understand what they are feeling. Throw a couple of 'what ifs' out there yourself and give them a worst-case scenario. Let's say, for example, that a customer says 'Well, it's not a big thing, really. I'm just not sure that I haven't seen this sweater for a better price.' A service person can respond 'Oh, I know the feeling. What if you find out you could have got it a little bit cheaper somewhere else? That bothers me every time I go shopping. Or, even worse, what if you buy it here and find it for 50 per cent off somewhere else?'

The salesperson has now created what is commonly known as a straw man – a scenario designed to be easily knocked down. The salesperson might accomplish this by saying 'Well, thankfully, in our shop we have a complete money-back guarantee, so if that happens you can bring it back in an instant.' Or, if it's true, you can say 'Well, I don't think you'll find a significant difference in price from shop to shop here' (with emphasis on the word 'significant'). Give it a moment to sink in, see if your indecisive customer is solemnly nodding his or her head and then proceed instantly with a solid assumed close: 'Now, would you like to look at the accessories that go with that?' Whatever you do, don't give the customer the opportunity to think of another 'what if?' Close the sale.

A common element of many sales training programmes is 'overcoming objections'. I think that 'objections' is a misleading term. Customers don't object to a product or to services, but they do have concerns about making poor purchase decisions. For indecisive customers, these concerns are very real, and it is important that you don't try to gloss over them.

2. You didn't close the sale

Customers who don't make decisions easily don't necessarily have indecisive personalities. Often they simply appear indecisive because the salesperson didn't close the sale. I have observed this scene hundreds of times: a salesperson conducts a perfect sales interview, right up to presenting the perfect product, and then stands there holding the product, waiting for the customer to say 'OK, I'll take it.' Because the salesperson is no longer in control of the situation, the customer wavers for a moment and then says 'Well, I'm going to think about it for a while...' The customer walks away, and the salesperson says 'I suppose the customer wasn't ready to buy yet.'

The easiest way of preventing indecisive behaviour is to make sure that you close every sale. Don't wait for the customer to do it.

Stressed-out Sally

A young salesperson related an interesting experience to me. A husband and wife entered her shop. She greeted them and asked if there was anything she could help them find. The woman said 'Paper clips. We need paper clips.' The salesperson took her to the paper clips, but the wife said 'No, I need bigger ones.' So the salesperson showed her the jumbo-sized paper clips, but the woman said 'No, I need some that are even bigger than that.' The salesperson apologized, said that her shop didn't carry them in any larger size, but she offered to see if they could be ordered.

Without warning, the woman suddenly burst into tears and said 'Our house just burnt down! It burnt down to the ground. My cat died.'

The salesperson responded 'Oh, how awful', and then waited a moment to see if there was any connection between this incident and the paper clips.

Suddenly, the woman whirled on the salesperson, shoved her face 2 inches from the salesperson's face, and snarled 'I told you my cat died!' The woman and her husband then turned and walked out of the shop.

Stress can do strange things to people. The greater the stress, the more strangely people behave. But unless customers are under stress that you have created, there is little you can really do about it. And although they may be behaving oddly, your customers don't really expect you to do anything about it. They aren't really blaming you for their problems – they simply need an outlet, and you happen to be handy.

The best response when this sort of thing happens is no response. You will only make matters worse.

Oblivious Oliver

Have you ever had the sensation that a customer is simply not listening to what you have to say? It's frustrating, but unfortunately it's also usually a self-inflicted problem. Often it happens because you are talking when you are supposed to be listening, and the customer has tuned you out. Few people actually listen long enough or well enough to have earned the right, in the customer's mind, to talk.

Having said this, however, there are some people who seem to be virtually incapable of listening. Some get ideas in their heads and can't seem to shake them no matter what you say.

A company once called my organization up and asked us to put together a training programme for its sales force to, in our prospective client's words, 'take us to the next level'. As we began the project, we did considerable research into the company's current needs and past endeavours. One of the things we found was a one-year-old, comprehensive customer survey. It confirmed what we had already begun to suspect – that the company still needed to wrestle down the basics before it could even begin to consider looking at the 'next level'.

We explained this situation to our client. We described the pyramid of training and how critical the foundation would be to long-term performance levels. We outlined cost–benefit models and showed where the greatest pay-off would be. We walked the client through his company's own research to show him the precise areas in which his people needed further development. We recommended that, based on all this information, we should put together a plan that worked on cementing the fundamentals into his company's culture. It would mean revisiting some skills in which his employees had already been trained, but they would be better prepared in future years for training in 'next-level' skills and concepts.

All the way through, our client nodded in vigorous agreement. Everything we said made sense. He couldn't wait to see our recommendation. When we returned the next week and presented it, however, our client said 'This is all very nice, but it's so basic. How is this supposed to take us to the next level?'

So we walked him through the theory of building a sound foundation of the basics again, and again we cited his own research as identifying the levels his people were at. We explained how the 'next level' wasn't realistic at this particular juncture. Again he nodded vehemently and agreed. Then he said 'But I really think they should go through advanced-level training.'

I remember thinking that this man may have been the stupidest person I'd ever met. It didn't matter how logically we presented information to the contrary; he wanted to take his people to the next level. The fact that he would be wasting his money was irrelevant. The fact that a higher-level programme would be ineffective was unimportant. It had to be advanced-level training. I struggled for a handle on the moment. Should we give him what he seemingly wanted and run the risk of an ill-advised and ineffective strategy damaging our reputation? Or should I just give him the names of a couple of other companies and suggest he call them? It was at that moment he let something slip out. 'Who knows, maybe we'll win another award', he said casually.

I had the glimmer of an idea, so I started to ask him some questions. It turned out that he was only six months into the job. There had been open dissension about him having been given the job over some other, internal candidates. On top of everything, his predecessor had won an award for the training programme the company had developed the year before. As it turned out, the programme had been focused on the fundamentals.

Now I was beginning to understand him. He wanted to prove that he was just as good as his predecessor, and he didn't want to appear as though he was just duplicating what had been done the year before. He wanted a higher-level training programme not because he thought his employees needed one, but because it would make him look like a more progressive and forward-thinking manager. While I didn't agree with his rationale, I at least now understood where he was coming from.

Where I was concerned with end results, he was concerned with how he would be perceived by his peers. So we revised our recommendation to include a sophisticated and high-profile performance measurement tool that he could hold up for everyone to see. The training was kept at a fundamental level. We were able to achieve the kinds of results we wanted, and he won his award – two, in fact.

When customers seem to be completely intent on not listening, not following logic or not adopting recommendations, and have no apparent reason for doing so, often the invisible wall you are hitting is a hidden agenda. The solution? Building trust, asking questions, listening carefully to the answers and not appearing judgemental when the truth comes out.

There are times, of course, when you will never get a straight answer. In this case, it's best not to second-guess your customer; instead, make your decisions based on your own integrity and that of your company.

Conclusion

Never let them see you sweat.

Well, that about covers it. We've addressed most of our Customers from Hell and even outlined some of the things to keep in mind so we don't become Service People from Hell. We've talked about unsatisfied customers and about how you can use the principles of LESTER to win them over and turn them into loyal customers. We've talked about some broad categories of unreasonable customers as well as some specific strategies for dealing with each type. We haven't covered them all, but let's face it – there are a lot of weird people out there. Even if you're armed with the best knowledge and are as prepared as you can be, chances are that sometime in your career you are going to be surprised by a customer with some new and inventive way to drive you mad.

Customer service is about people. Life is about people. And, more often than not, the difference between our successes and our failures hinges on the strength of our communication skills. The wonderful thing about customer contact occupations is that they give us an opportunity to hone our communication skills every day. We learn how to develop relationships and how to make people feel good about themselves. We learn how to work with customers, peers and superiors. We learn how much of an impact one person can have on the lives of others.

Dealing effectively with conflict and confrontation is both a communication skill and a lifestyle choice. When you're faced with conflict, you have only three choices: you can try to resolve it, you can try to win it or you can try to run from it. This book has focused on the first option. Earlier on in the book, I asked 'What is more important – ending a war or winning a war?' It's an important question, and you should be frank with yourself in answering it, because the communication skills you require for each option are quite different.

I can promise you that mastering the skills for resolving conflict will serve you well throughout your life. As you perfect these skills, you will earn people's respect, trust and confidence. I've never heard anyone say 'I hate that woman; she's always finding positive solutions to conflict.' My guess is that, if you had the patience to read this book, then you are probably willing to practise the techniques I've outlined. If you do, you will find that there are fewer and fewer situations you can't handle. For those occasional ones that still stump you, remember these famous words from the days of vaudeville: never let them see you sweat.